CORPORATE TAX HARMONISATION AND ECONOMIC EFFICIENCY

Michael Devereux and Mark Pearson

The Institute for Fiscal Studies
180/182 Tottenham Court Road
London W1P 9LE

Published by
The Institute for Fiscal Studies
180/182 Tottenham Court Road
London W1P 9LE
(Tel. 01-636 3784)

Distributed by
Woodhead-Faulkner (Publishers) Ltd
Simon & Schuster International Group
Fitzwilliam House
32 Trumpington Street
Cambridge CB2 1QY

© The Institute for Fiscal Studies, October 1989
ISBN 0 902992 80 5

Typeset and printed by
Parchment (Oxford) Ltd
60 Hurst Street
Oxford OX4 1HD

PREFACE

The authors are grateful to a number of companies which have financially supported the research reported here. They are Allied Lyons, Bass, BAT, Beecham, BP, British Telecom, Grand Metropolitan, ICI, Marks and Spencer, Price Waterhouse and RTZ. We are also grateful to a number of individuals from these firms, especially Paul Bowes, Ken Etherington, Hugh Roe and Michael Whitear. Harold Freeman, Malcolm Gammie, John Kay, Michael Keen, Colin Mayer, Tricia Rennie, Bill Robinson, Stephen Smith and Robert Weedon have all offered useful help and advice. In addition, we would like to thank Edmund Crooks and Charles Wookey for their contributions to the early part of the project, and Chantal Crevel-Robinson and Pat Francis who prepared the manuscript for publication. The opinions expressed in the report are, however, those of the authors alone. They are not necessarily those of the sponsors, nor of the individuals named, nor of the IFS, which has no corporate views.

Michael Devereux is Director of the Corporate Sector Programme at the Institute for Fiscal Studies.

Mark Pearson is a Research Officer at the Institute for Fiscal Studies.

CONTENTS

INTRODUCTION AND SUMMARY

By agreeing not to act in their own narrowly-defined interests and instead acting for the collective good, it is possible that countries can end up being better off than they could have been had they acted selfishly. Few would argue with this as a general proposition. The difficulty is in deciding whether it applies in particular cases. This report attempts to illuminate the discussion as to whether there is a need to apply it in the case of corporate taxes. Specifically, should the European Community harmonise its corporation taxes?

Differences in corporate tax regimes between countries can lead to several technical problems. For example, various rules regarding 'transfer pricing' (the price at which different companies in the same group sell goods to each other) and 'thin capitalisation' (the extent to which they lend to each other) are designed to reduce the degree to which groups can arrange their affairs so as to earn their profit in a low tax country. Mergers between companies from different countries can sometimes be complicated by tax issues. In particular, it is possible for the merged firm to pay more tax than the two separate entities. These technical problems may be administratively costly, and may sometimes impede efficient business practice. They do not, however, make an overwhelming case for harmonisation. The costs involved seem unlikely to justify the political upheaval of removing the right of sovereign states to set their own tax regimes.

A stronger case for corporate tax harmonisation rests on the following two propositions: 'if tax rates differ between countries, companies will sometimes be tempted to invest in the low tax country, even though it may cost more to produce there', and 'if tax rates on two companies differ, one company may be able to sell its goods more cheaply than its competitor, even though its production costs are higher'. The existence of a tax incentive for companies to locate an investment in one country rather than another constitutes an absence of capital export neutrality (CEN). The existence of a purely tax-induced competitive advantage of a company in one country over another from a different country constitutes an absence of capital import neutrality (CIN).

The importance of CEN depends on the costs of production in different locations. If these were identical in two different countries, then a tax incentive to locate in one of the countries is unimportant, in the sense that no resources would be wasted by investing in one rather than the other. Resources would only be wasted if production were cheaper in the higher tax country but in fact took place in the

6

lower tax country because of the tax advantage. Similarly with CIN: if two companies were equally efficient, the fact that one company was able to gain a larger market share because it was taxed at a lower rate and could therefore sell at a lower price would not waste resources. Only if a more efficient company were displaced by a less efficient one would resources be wasted.

The existence of economic advantages which are specific to particular locations in the absence of tax is therefore necessary for there to be a tax-induced inefficient allocation of resources in Europe. These economic advantages generally give rise to economic rents — profits over and above the minimum required by a company in order to undertake a project. A location specific economic rent may occur in the country of production (the *source* country), for example, because the workers in that country are more efficient, or because transport costs are lower. A location specific rent may also occur in the country in which the the parent company is resident (the *residence* country). Suppose that a company can earn an economic rent in the absence of tax simply because it is more efficient than any competitors, or because it owns the patents to a more efficient production process: if the company were free to change its residence then, other things being equal, it would move to a low-tax country. However, in fact it is often very difficult or impossible for companies to do this and so the economic rent earned from their efficiency or patent may be location specific.

Economic inefficiencies of the kind described could therefore be avoided if governments constrained themselves to tax only the location specific economic rents which arise in their country. However, no corporate tax regime limits itself in this way and in practical terms it would be impossible for it to do so. In the absence of such regimes, but in the presence of some location specific economic rents, CEN could only be achieved if each company faced the same effective tax rate irrespective of the location of its investment. CIN could only be achieved if all companies operating in a particular market faced the same effective tax rate. If CIN or CEN were introduced more goods could be made with the same resources: Europe as a whole would be better off. This is the more convincing case that can be made in favour of corporate tax harmonisation.

One other factor commonly thought to be important in discussion of corporate tax harmonisation is equity. That is that each national government should receive a 'fair' allocation of tax revenue from profits earned in its country or by residents of its country. However, there is no economic reason for describing any particular allocation

7

of revenues as 'fair'. It is more realistic to describe any allocation as needing to be politically acceptable. In any case, the ultimate revenue received by a government may be independent of whether it has the right to impose its own preferred tax regime on either activities which take place in its country or on companies resident in its country. This is because the distribution between source and residence countries of the total tax revenue collected by them can be determined independently of the amount collected by one country transferring some of the tax revenue it raises to the other. The fact that economic efficiency may dictate that a particular country should determine the tax regime faced by a certain company therefore does not mean that another country should not receive a share of the revenue raised.

Making a theoretical case for corporate tax harmonisation is insufficient to justify a change from the status quo. Two further steps are required. First, it must be shown that capital import and capital export neutrality do not currently exist. Second, it must be shown that their absence actually affects the behaviour of firms.

In Chapter 2, a model is developed which estimates effective tax rates on investment. It considers a parent company, resident in one member state, which invests through a wholly-owned subsidiary in another member state. The investment is in an 'average' basket of assets — a mixture of commercial and industrial buildings, and plant and machinery. The subsidiary is wholly equity financed by the parent, which, in turn, may raise finance by borrowing, issuing new equity or retaining earnings. The subsidiary remits all its profits back to the parent, in the form of dividends. The basic model has been widely used in other contexts, but is extended here to consider transnational tax rates, and estimate the effective average rate of tax on economic rent as well as the effective marginal tax rate on marginal investments.

The model illustrates the complexity of the current system of taxing transnational investments. Profits are taxed firstly in the country where they are made; there is often a second tax, a withholding tax, levied when profits leave the country in which they were generated. There may be yet another tax levied on the parent's profits — including those made overseas — by the residence country. This describes only the most straightforward case — far more complicated tax arrangements can and do exist.

It would be suprising if such a convoluted tax system resulted in economic efficiency, and indeed the model confirms that: there is no

CEN or CIN within Europe. A British firm operating in the absence of any corporate taxes might earn a return on its investment such that it could provide its financiers with a return 75 per cent higher by investing in one country rather than another, but in fact would still prefer the country in which it earned the lower pre-tax return because of its lower taxes. The dispersion of tax rates and the amount of distortion produced by taxes increases with inflation. Another feature of the international tax system which the model illustrates is that a country may have a comparatively low tax rate when economic rent is low, but a comparitively high rate if economic rent is high (or vice versa).

The model decomposes the dispersion of 'effective' marginal and average tax rates into its constituent parts. Somewhat surprisingly, differences in the tax base and the statutory tax rate between countries independently make only a small contribution to the dispersion. By contrast, withholding taxes on profits flowing from one country to another are responsible for a larger part of the dispersion. Indeed, the abolition of withholding taxes and the standardisation of the treatment of foreign source income throughout Europe proves to be almost as effective in reducing the dispersion as the European Commission's far more radical plan of harmonising tax rates and the treatment of dividends together with the abolition of withholding taxes and the exemption of foreign source income from tax.

Chapter 3 reports the results of a survey of British business conducted by the IFS and distributed by the Confederation of British Industry. This survey attempted to find out how important tax was in certain business decisions. Three topics were addressed. First was the question of the importance of tax incentives to companies' decisions concerning where to locate an investment. The second was the influence tax has on business structures. The third was whether the respondents think that corporate tax harmonisation is desirable.

The results suggest that tax does influence decisions about where to locate. Of those companies who answered the questionnaire and who had overseas investment, all thought that tax was *sometimes* a relevant consideration when deciding in which country to locate an investment, nearly half thought it to be *always* a relevant consideration, and over 40 per cent thought tax to be at least *usually* a major factor in such decisions.

In addition the financial structure of operations appears to be even more influenced by differential taxation. Companies use branches and subsidiaries to optimise their international tax situation. The decision as to how to finance a project — whether to raise the money in the country of production or not, whether and how the parent should fund its branch or subsidiary and whether borrowing or retained earnings should be used — is substantially determined by tax considerations. Companies repatriate profits from overseas investments through opaque business structures in order to reduce tax.

Perhaps surprisingly, given the UK's relatively low tax rate on corporate profits, the respondents overwhelmingly supported the principle of corporate tax harmonisation. They believe that tax should not be permitted to distort decisions as to in which European country to locate an investment. A rather smaller majority believes that non-European companies should also be allowed to benefit from such a level playing field. Similar majorities were found in favour of the proposition that competing companies should face the same effective tax rate no matter what their nationality. More concretely, large majorities were found in favour of harmonisation of tax rates, of the tax treatment of dividends, of the tax base, and of the tax treatment of foreign source income.

The final chapter of this report considers how best to achieve a better European corporate tax system. There is a trade-off between the achievement of economic neutrality and maintaining the right of member states to set their own tax regimes. Having said that, there are many reforms which improve economic efficiency but which continue to permit member states to set their own tax regime for 'domestic' business — companies which are owned and which operate in one country. Much improvement could be made without removing this form of national sovereignty. In view of some member states' reluctance to give up any sovereignty, this suggests that the Commission's proposals to harmonise the tax base and tax rates should not be a priority.

One interesting approach to reform is to consider the levying of corporation tax according to the residence of the parent company, rather than the current mixture of mainly source based tax but with some aspects of residence based taxation. This achieves capital export neutrality — wherever a company invested in Europe it would pay the same rate of tax. It would leave countries with the right to tax domestic companies at whatever rate they wished. The proposal requires that the residence country taxes the Europe-wide profits of companies, giving full credit for taxes paid in the source country. This need not require a radical redistribution of corporate tax revenues between member states; the allocation of the tax revenue between countries is a separate matter, which can be determined by mutual agreement. If this European-wide basis of assessment were adopted, complex anti-tax avoidance provisions to deal with problems such as transfer pricing and thin capitalisation would no longer be required within Europe. Depending on the exact system of this type chosen, however, there may be some increase in the administrative costs.

Even if this approach is rejected, several other reforms would be worthwhile. One is to extend current British treatment of transnational flows throughout Europe — abolishing withholding taxes on payment of dividends and interest abroad and giving credit against tax on foreign source income for source country taxes to the extent that they are no greater than the residence country liability. This would substantially improve the degree of capital export neutrality within Europe. A partial credit system *with averaging* would be even more effective in promoting capital export neutrality — instead of comparing the residence tax liability with each source country separately, foreign taxes would be pooled and the residence country tax rate compared with the average of foreign tax rates.

At the minimum, withholding taxes should be abolished. The model described in Chapter 2 shows that they alone account for a substantial amount of the dispersion in effective tax rates in Europe. They raise relatively little revenue — only being levied when profits are repatriated to shareholders or debtholders in another country. They can have only one effect — to tax foreign-owned companies more heavily than domestic companies. It is, perhaps, surprising that over thirty years after the signing of the Treaty of Rome such blatant discrimination continues.

An objection is sometimes made to corporate tax harmonisation on the grounds that whatever convergence is necessary will be achieved by the pressure of market forces. This objection has some truth, but should be treated with care. First, the incentive structure for governments may be complex and need not necessarily lead member states to take action which would reduce distortions. For example, there is some incentive for governments to have a low basic corporate tax rate in order to give domestic companies a competitive advantage, to impose high withholding taxes on profits repatriated to countries operating credit systems but low or zero withholding taxes on profits repatriated to countries exempting foreign source income. Second, a belief in market forces is *not* equivalent to saying that nothing needs to be done. Market forces have not led to the abolition of withholding taxes which lead to large distortions in Europe — indeed, market forces would be more powerful if withholding taxes had been abolished. Third, a tax system which was the outcome of market forces might not be the one which governments would choose. For example, governments might need continually to cut tax rates (or increase grants) in order to encourage (or maintain) net inward investment. In principle, a lower bound to corporate tax regimes would be necessary, although it would be very difficult to define.

In summary, the political need for sovereignty can be reconciled with greater economic efficiency. The solution is to remove the distortions in the tax treatment of transnational investments within Europe. This can lead to large gains in terms of economic efficiency, yet continues to allow national governments to maintain complete sovereignty over most corporate activity, which takes place only domestically. A case could be made on economic grounds for more far-reaching reforms but, at least at the moment, such reforms would be likely to remain on the drawing board in the face of concern about national sovereignty.

CHAPTER 1

EFFICIENCY AND CORPORATE TAX HARMONISATION

Persuading twelve countries to drop the quirks, anomalies, accumulated case laws and national preferences that together make up a tax system, in favour of a common basis of assessment and similar rates, is hardly a simple task. This is the case with all taxes, as the right to raise revenue is seen as being close to the very essence of sovereignty. Small wonder that governments of sovereign countries are sensitive to suggestions that tax systems should be altered to suit the wishes of other states, even when the changes are reciprocal.

Nevertheless, it seems quite likely that some sort of limited agreement on indirect tax administration and possibly rates may well take place by 1992. However, getting agreement among the European Community countries to reform their tax systems will be harder in the case of corporate tax[1] than for indirect taxes. First, it is much harder to clarify the purposes of corporate tax harmonisation than for indirect tax harmonisation. This is not to say that the need to harmonise is any less in the case of corporate taxes, in fact the reverse is probably true; just that the reasons for harmonisation are more subtle, and it is difficult to translate them into realistic practical changes from the current situation. Second, companies have adapted themselves to the existing tax structures; changing these will tend to disrupt the locational, administrative and financial decisions of far more companies than most changes to indirect taxes.[2] Much of this report will address these two issues, isolating the case for harmonisation of taxes and attempting to determine whether the current situation is so bad that governments should indeed, despite their misgivings, agree among themselves some ground rules about how companies operating in, or owned by residents of, their countries should be taxed.

Both the economic and institutional prospects for Europe in the 1990s have been transformed by the Single European Act and the drive to complete the European Internal Market. The European Commission has recently made proposals for the harmonisation of the corporate tax base, (Commission, 1988) and has suggested that this be considered in tandem with an earlier proposal to harmonise the corporate tax system and tax rates (Commission, 1975). However, the harmonisation of corporate taxation is not specifically part of the 1992 programme. This report will argue that there may be a stronger case on economic grounds for harmonising, or at least coordinating, corporate taxes than for indirect tax harmonisation. It will also argue that even if the single market is completed without any change to the current situation, the pressure for action will grow after 1992, because once all other obstacles are removed or reduced, the distortionary effects of uncoordinated corporate taxes will become both more apparent and more important.

1.1 The Economic Case for Harmonisation

This report assesses the economic, as opposed to the political, case for harmonisation. Two factors are often stressed: fairness (who should get what share of total corporate taxes raised in Europe) and economic efficiency (how large will be the amount of profits that are available to be taxed). As the discussion below makes clear, fairness is of little relevance to corporate tax harmonisation. The key to understanding the rationale for corporate taxation is efficiency. It is important to be clear at the outset that we are concerned with efficiency on a European-wide basis. We do not discuss the policies which a national government, interested only in the welfare of its own citizens (possibly to the detriment of others), should follow. Rather we are interested in the economic gains which the European Community as a whole might derive from harmonising its corporate taxes.

Fairness

When a company manufactures and sells in the same member state in which its owners also reside, it seems clear that it is the government of that country which is entitled to levy taxes on corporate profits. The British government — and *only* the British government — will tax a company which manufactures and sells in the UK, and which is ultimately owned in the UK. But suppose that a British registered company owns a French subsidiary which sells in Italy, and the parent is itself owned by individuals residing in all parts of Europe. Which government should receive the tax on the profits of the subsidiary? At present, the French government would tax the operation on the basis of profits recorded under French corporate law; on the transfer of profits back to the UK the French would levy a further withholding tax; if the tax paid in France were less than would have been charged had production been in Britain then under the credit system there may be a further British liability on the dividends repatriated to Britain. When the British parent distributes the profits, advanced corporation tax (ACT) will be paid, which may or may not be fully relieved, depending on whether most profits were made abroad or not, and the various income tax administrations of the countries where the shareholders live will each take a share of the income.

'Fairness' plays little role in all of this. One concern of states is to collect as much revenue as they can from companies, regardless of where operations occur. The government of the *source* country (the country where goods are actually manufactured) gets the first chance to tax profits, so usually takes most. These acquisitive tendencies are limited only by the fear of incentives to manufacture in that country being eroded, and the possibility that if foreign owned concerns are taxed too highly, there may be some retaliatory action against domestically owned operations abroad. The *residence* country (the country in which the parent company is based) tends to take less tax, simply because the profit has already been taxed at least once, so there is less of it left. However, even supposing that all the member states of the Community, or, indeed, of the world community, agreed to act fairly, it is not clear what a fair system would be.

Companies may hand money to tax authorities, but they do not bear the true burden of the taxes; ultimately only individuals can do so. Insofar as corporate taxes are reflected in the value of the returns to shareholders' equity, in the price of the good or service bought by consumers, and in the wages of the work force, then these groups bear the tax burden. Yet these groups may not live in the country of production. Even if the share of the tax burden accruing to each of these groups could be identified we are not much further towards a concept of a fair allocation of revenue. The traditional debates regarding the allocation of tax are concerned with the distribution of tax payments among individuals within a jurisdiction. However, such considerations do not offer much insight into the two issues of whether two equal shareholders (German and British) of a French company operating primarily in Italy and selling in Spain should bear a similar tax burden and which government or governments should receive the revenue.

In particular, it should be noted that, in principle, even if tax should be in some way identified with benefits received, this offers virtually no practical guidance. The so-called 'benefit' principle which is sometimes invoked as an approach to a fair allocation of revenue between governments is useless for practical purposes. This would argue that, for example, production activities gain the benefit of freely provided public goods in the host country — roads and other transport facilities, for example — and may in addition impose costs in the form of pollution. The host country in which the production activities take place should capture the highest share of total tax revenue in order to compensate it for these benefits and costs. This, of course, ignores the benefits which these activities bring to the host country, for example the additional employment created. It is extremely difficult to assess the costs and benefits of any particular operation. To try to use such principles to design a 'fair' tax system which could apply to all such investments is not only administratively impossible, it is conceptually impossible, simply because costs and benefits will vary between different projects.

The absence of any clear principle as to which government should receive the revenue does not imply, of course, that individual governments will not wish to secure as high a share of the total tax on a unit of profit as possible. In the above example each of the three or more governments might claim some part of the tax on profits. What a harmonised tax system requires is therefore a set of rules governing allocation which is *acceptable* to member governments. The point here is that such an allocation cannot reflect any precise notion of equity, but simply arbitrary political judgement. The concept of 'fairness' cannot be used to justify tax harmonisation.

Efficiency

Corporate taxation can affect the efficiency of economic activity in numerous ways — for example, which projects companies invest in and where and when they do so, and the ways in which they raise finance. To varying degrees, these problems are common to all corporate tax systems. The specifically European problems are of two sorts. One is that the existence of separate revenue authorities inhibits European-wide rationalisation of business structures. For instance, trans-frontier mergers involving UK companies can result in increased tax liabilities, because of the problem of unrelieved ACT.

The second and more general group of problems of corporate taxation inhibiting European economic efficiency concerns the question 'who does what where?'. There are two sorts of efficiency that are important, the 'where' and the 'who'. For there to be efficiency, an investment must be located in the area which results in production at minimum cost, and it must be done by the company which can do the project at minimum cost.

Capital export neutrality and capital import neutrality.

Capital export neutrality, or CEN, concerns the decision about *where* to invest. All other factors being equal, a company is likely to invest in the place which gives the highest after-tax profit. In the absence of any tax, then the location of an investment will be in the country where production (broadly defined to include transport costs) is cheapest. If taxes make investment in that country more expensive than production would be in another country, the consequence may be that investment takes place elsewhere. This would result in a waste of resources, from the point of view of the Community as a whole.

> **Example.** Suppose that Ford decides to expand capacity in Europe. The car it wishes to produce will retail for £5000. If it invests in Germany, each car would cost £3000 to produce; if it does so in Spain the cost would be £3500. However, the German government charges £1200 tax on the profits made by selling each car, whereas the Spanish revenue authorities extract only £500. In neither case will any other taxes be paid. Ford therefore locates its investment in Spain, and £500 of resources are wasted for each car built. There is no capital export neutrality.

For CEN to be attained, a company must face the same effective tax rate wherever it invests.

In the case of capital import neutrality, or CIN, the focus is on *who* invests. In the absence of tax, competition should ensure that the eventual investor is the one who can produce goods most cheaply. If taxes discriminate between companies, then it is possible that a less efficient producer may end up undertaking a project because a more efficient competitor is taxed more heavily. Again, resources are not being used as efficiently as is possible.

> **Example.** Suppose that a new bridge is to be built over the Thames. The project is put out to competitive tender. In the absence of any taxes, Saint-Gobain would put in the lowest bid of £50 million, as it could build the bridge at the lowest cost. However, the French government decides to tax Saint-Gobain on its worldwide profits in addition to any tax that the UK charges. In order to be able to earn an adequate profit for its shareholders, Saint-Gobain has to raise its bid to £60 million. Wimpey, not subject to the additional French tax, has its bid of £55 million accepted. The bridge is built at a cost £5 million in excess of what it needed to be. In this case, there is no capital import neutrality.

For CIN to be attained, all companies potentially able to produce some good must face the same effective tax rate, no matter what nationality the producing company is. It is important to note that CIN requires that the profit being made on goods sold in a particular market is taxed at the same rate. The 'bridge' example above is a special case, in that the bridge is produced and consumed in the same place. For most goods this need not be the case; for instance, cars can be produced in one country and exported to another. For CIN to be attained, cars produced by Peugeot and Fiat in France and Italy to be sold in the UK must face the same effective tax rate as cars produced domestically by Nissan or The Rover Group.

Location specific rents.

The examples given above referred to companies being *more efficient* than other companies. If all companies were equally efficient, then different effective European tax rates would not result in any loss of economic welfare on a European-wide basis. The fact that the French tax rate were higher than the Italian tax rate might mean that all cars in Europe would be produced by Fiat, and that Peugeot would fail to sell any cars at all. However, no resources would be wasted. Peugeot could not produce those cars at a lower cost. Similarly, if all investment locations were equally efficient, the fact that the Spanish tax rate were lower than the German one would matter to no-one bar the Germans, who might lose all their corporate tax revenue as all companies located in Spain. In general, if no company or location is more efficient than any other, there can be no *welfare loss*, measured in European terms, if taxes cause one company or investment location to be favoured over any others.

When one company is more efficient than its competitors, then for a given final price it is possible that it will earn more profit. Assuming that the other companies are earning a *normal* rate of profit (sufficient to give the providers of finance an adequate return on their capital, but no more) then the efficient company may earn *super-normal* profits, commonly known as economic rent, or just *rent*. The concept of rent, and the existence of rent in practice, is crucial to an understanding of the international aspects of corporation taxes.

Tax is only paid when companies invest in projects on which they expect to earn a rent. If, in the absence of tax, companies expected to earn only the bare minimum required to satisfy their shareholders or debtholders who provide the capital for the project, any positive tax burden would reduce the after-tax profit to below this minimum necessary level, and so the project would not be worthwhile. Only if companies earn more than this minimum will they be able to pay tax and still satisfy their shareholders. In other words, there must be rents for companies to be able to afford to pay corporate taxes and hence for governments to be able to collect any corporate tax revenues at all.

However, if a firm could locate itself and its investment *anywhere*, and still earn the same level of rent before tax, then a unilateral decision by one country to introduce a higher corporate tax than all other countries would result in that company locating and producing outside of that country. In the extreme case in which all companies were in such a position, that government would receive no revenue from its corporation tax.

Given that not all tax systems are identical, tax is received by governments because of the existence of *location specific rents*. Companies locate themselves or their investments in countries which take some of their profits as tax. They locate in such countries, because otherwise they would not earn as much rent post-tax. The tax can only be avoided if the rent is given up. Countries in which location specific rents are located can therefore tax those rents.

There are three sources of location specific rents — consumption, production, and residence.

(1) Consumption

If the inhabitants of a country particularly like a product, they may be prepared to pay more than its cost in order to get it. A rent can be earned by the companies producing that good. It is location specific because the product has to be sold to consumers of that country in order to earn the rent. If the company stopped supplying the country, its world-wide rent would fall. Hence that part of its rent is specific to that country.

> **Example.** Suppose that UK consumers are willing to pay 40p for a can of Coca-Cola, although it only costs 10p to make. A rent of 30p can therefore be earned. How this rent is taxed depends on the actions of the Inland Revenue and of Coca-Cola. For instance, suppose Coca-Cola produces its cans in the USA and sells them through a wholly-owned UK subsidiary. The Inland Revenue could apply an arms length pricing principle to deem that the price paid by the subsidiary was 10p: the subsidiary would thus be deemed to have earned the 30p rent, and the UK would collect some tax on this rent. If the Inland Revenue did not take this action,

then Coca-Cola could claim that all its rent was earned in the US, and would pay only US tax.[3]

(2) Production

This is the easiest source of location specific rents to understand. For whatever reason, it is often cheaper to produce goods and services in one country rather than in another. At one extreme is oil — this can only be extracted by producing where the oil is. It cannot be extracted by locating a production plant in another country simply because the tax rate is lower. It is because oil production is so very location specific that the UK government can charge higher tax rates on oil production than on most other production. Note that other taxes can *cause* a location specific rent (for example, income taxes may influence the cost of labour; property taxes the cost of buildings).

> **Example.** Steel requires coal and iron as raw materials. Both tend to be rather bulky, so transport costs are high. Producing in the same country as that in which the raw materials are mined results in lower transport costs, and hence a location specific rent compared with producing elsewhere. As a consequence, nearly all steel production is done near coal- or iron-fields.

(3) Residence

Companies are incorporated in some country. If some companies are more efficient than others, the effect is that rent is earned by a company which is attached to a specific country. Rent is not earned *because* the company is registered in a particular country (although it is possible to think of reasons such as legal protection and prestige as to why companies might earn some small rent by incorporating in a particular country) but rent is nevertheless earned in a specific location.

> **Example.** ICI is a UK resident company. Suppose that because of superior management it can operate any given piece of technology more efficiently than its German competitors. This is a residence location specific rent because only ICI can earn that rent. Note that it is irrelevant where the activity actually takes place. Another source of such a rent is a patent. If ICI holds exclusive rights to a new paint making process, it may produce it more efficiently than Hoechst or Bayer. ICI therefore earns a rent. The rent accrues to a company because of its efficiency, but the

company is attached to a country, and so the rent can reasonably be termed 'location specific'. Therefore the British government can impose a corporate tax without forcing the company out of business.

This raises the question as to whether such companies can change their country of residence in order to reduce their tax. In the UK at least, such a move is not easy. Until 1988, it was a *criminal* offence for a UK company to change its residence without permission from the Treasury. Currently, the UK situation depends on the type of residence which a company has. UK incorporated businesses cannot emigrate under any circumstances — as proved when the Daily Mail tried to change its residence to the Netherlands. The European Court (Case 81/87, 27 September, 1988) ruled that there was no legal right for a company incorporated in a country to transfer its residency to another Community country, which effectively prevents emigration. It is possible to be incorporated in another country but to be deemed a UK resident if central management and control is in the UK.[4] Such a company could only change its residence by moving its central management and control. Even in this case it would be required to pay capital gains tax on any increase on the value of its assets since their acquisition.

CEN, CIN and location specific rents.

It is the relationship between location specific rents and whether income is taxed at source or residence which determines whether CIN and CEN are achieved. Suppose that tax systems were sufficiently well co-ordinated so that tax was levied only at source (where production takes place). If there were perfect capital mobility and, in an extreme case, there were no *production* location specific rents, then, in global terms, the absence of capital export neutrality would not matter. If one country taxed companies investing there at a higher rate than those same companies would be taxed if they invested in another country, all would actually invest in the other country. The high tax country would receive no tax revenue, but that would be its problem. No resources would be used inefficiently, because efficiency does not in this case depend on the production location.

However, if there *were* production location specific rents, the higher tax rate could begin to distort competition — companies might be tempted to invest elsewhere, despite being able to earn a higher *pre-tax* return in the high tax country.

Example. Suppose that in deciding where in Europe to build a new assembly plant, Ford finds that all countries are equally attractive. However, the effective tax rate in Germany proves to be higher than that in Ireland. It therefore locates its plant in Ireland. No resources are wasted by Ford making this decision, because in the absence of tax, all locations are equally desirable. Ford then decides to make a high-performance engine in Europe. Suppose that this time the higher efficiency of German engineers means that pre-tax costs are lower (and hence pre-tax profits are higher) if the engines are made in Germany. However, given the high effective rate of tax, this investment is also made in Ireland. In this case, more resources are used than is necessary and there is a welfare loss (in European terms, although not necessarily for the Irish), corresponding to the absence of capital export neutrality.

If taxes are levied only at source, but rents are *residence* location specific, the higher tax in Germany would not be important. Both efficient and less-efficient companies would avoid the high tax country, but no resources would be wasted.

Example. Suppose that Fiat is more efficient than Ford. If they both located an engine plant in Germany, Fiat would produce the engines at a lower cost. But the same is true if they both located in Ireland. If tax is levied on a source basis, and German tax is higher than Irish tax, both Ford and Fiat may locate in Ireland. Fiat would still produce its engines more cheaply than Ford. There is no welfare loss if tax is source based and there are only residence location specific rents.

At the other extreme is the situation where taxes are levied according to the location of company residence, regardless of where production actually takes place. In this case, production specific rents do *not* result in a distortion. If it is cheaper to produce in one country rather than elsewhere, companies will invest there, regardless of whether their own government takes 20 per cent or 80 per cent of the rent they generate. However, in this case, if rents are residence location specific, different tax rates may affect the minimum price which companies must charge in order to get an adequate return on capital.

Example. Suppose that Germany takes a high proportion of Volkswagen's profits, regardless of whether the profits are generated in Germany or in the UK. By contrast, suppose that the UK takes a much smaller portion of whatever profits The Rover Group makes, wherever it makes them. Assume Volkswagen to be the more efficient company. However, because it is taxed at a lower rate, The Rover Group can set prices which are not inflated by tax by as much as those set by Volkswagen. In this case, Rover will capture a larger share of the market than its efficiency dictates it should. There is a European-wide welfare loss corresponding to the absence of capital import neutrality.

Table 1.1 summarises the situation.

TABLE 1.1

Efficiency implications of interactions between tax systems and sources of location specific rent

Location Specific Rent Based on	Tax System Based on	
	Source	Residence
Production	Absence of CEN	Economically efficient
Residence	Economically efficient	Absence of CIN

Note that if the location specific rent is very high, the difference in the effective tax rate has to be correspondingly high for a company to be persuaded to locate an investment in a less efficient area, or for the less efficient company to attract more market share. Firms with moderate rents are more likely to have their behaviour influenced by the tax system than those with large rents.

CEN or CIN?

It is possible to make a case that *both* CEN *and* CIN are required for the aims of the 1992 programme not to be subverted by differences in corporate tax burdens. The creation of a single market in goods requires that producers should be able to produce anywhere in Europe to sell anywhere in Europe, unencumbered by national restrictions. Yet if companies can produce their goods cheaper than other equally (or even more) efficient competitors because of the corporate tax system, then there is no level playing field in the Single European Market. If all the benefits of a unified goods market are to be exploited, then all companies selling in any one country must face the same tax burden, regardless of whether the goods are produced in that country or are imported from another member state, and regardless of who owns the company. This principle of neutrality (the '1992 principle') requires both CEN and CIN.

The only way to get the 1992 principle of neutrality is by having identical effective tax burdens on all competing European businesses. This probably requires identical tax systems, rates and bases in each country. Even having these would be insufficient if losses made in one country could not be offset against profits made in another. Of course economic efficiency is not the only criterion by which movement towards harmonisation will be judged. Other factors, such as the giving up of sovereignty and administrative difficulties may therefore force a judgment as to the relative importance of CEN and CIN. Although these issues are discussed at length in Chapter 4 it is worth noting briefly here the cases in which CEN and CIN do and do not hold. If taxes are residence based CEN always holds. If taxes are source based CIN always holds. Thus the two ideals press the reformer in opposite directions, towards source or residence based taxes.

It may be that achieving CEN is more important than achieving CIN. The reason for believing this to be the case is because it seems likely that the advantages of investing in one location rather than another are greater than the differences in efficiency between competing firms. In other words, production location specific rents are more prevalent than residence location specific rents. If this is true, the choice between moving towards a source or residence base for a harmonised tax system should be in favour of a residence base. Inefficiencies would only then arise in cases in which rents depended on the location of residence.

Portfolio investment

The discussion has so far been concerned with taxes and incentives at the corporate level. However, when commentators talk about the 'free flow of capital' across national boundaries within Europe, they are often concerned with the location of portfolio investment by individuals and financial institutions. The main concern here is that tax regimes should not affect investors' decisions as to in which European company they buy shares. We call this form of neutrality 'shareholder capital export neutrality', or shareholder CEN.

The welfare loss which might arise through the absence of shareholder CEN is, in fact, the same as that which arises from the absence of CIN; that is, that a less efficient company may gain through a tax advantage over a more efficient company. If taxes at the corporate level were the same throughout Europe, then it would still be possible for, say, Fiat's shareholders to face a higher tax rate than Peugot's. To the extent that the companies take personal taxes into account in their activities, this would give Peugot a competitive advantage. This would clearly be the case if Fiat's sharehoders faced a higher tax rate simply because they had invested in Fiat, but this should properly be described as a tax on Fiat.

More generally, there are two ways in which shareholder CEN might not be attained even if all corporation taxes in Europe were the same. Both arise because countries may discriminate between domestic and foreign shareholders. First, withholding taxes may be charged on dividends and interest paid abroad. Second, the tax credit available to domestic shareholders under an imputation system may not be available to non-resident shareholders. Either of these cases might result in a welfare loss due to the absence of CEN, although the mechanisms by which this would occur are subtle. Basically, shareholders might be expected to arrange their affairs such that the post-tax return they earn from investments in different countries is the same. If these post-tax returns are affected by tax, the funds will be diverted towards the domestic economy, where they are likely to earn a lower return than could have been earned elsewhere. Of course, if this happens, there will be corresponding switches of investment all over Europe. Only in special circumstances, however, would the outcome be the same as in the absence of tax. If it is not the same, the welfare loss which arises is due to some companies gaining an advantage over their competitors. This similarity between CIN and shareholder CEN allows us to concentrate on just one: we mainly discuss CIN in this report.

1.2 Harmonisation: What Has Been the Strategy?

The history of corporate tax harmonisation in the European Community is a long and inglorious one. No directive of any substance has been adopted.

In the early 1960s, a committee (Neumark, 1963) suggested a split-rate corporate tax system, with distributed profits being taxed at a lower rate. In 1967, the Commission published a programme advocating a single corporate tax system (Commission, 1967). By 1971, another report had proposed a classical corporate tax system (Van den Tempel, 1971). During 1975 the Commission proposed a partial imputation system, with tax rates between 45 and 55 per cent (Commission, 1975). However, the draft directive made no proposal on the appropriate corporate tax *base*. By 1979, the European

Parliament still had not given its opinion on the 1975 proposal, and formally suspended its consideration until a tax base proposal was provided. The need for such a directive was acknowledged in 1980 (Commission, 1980), but a draft was not produced until 1988 (Commission, 1988a). In the interim, a series of three directives dating from 1969 and 1976 were reintroduced to the Council by the Commission, covering trans-border mergers (Commission, 1969a), parent-subsidiary relations (Commission 1969b), and the elimination of double taxation on transfer pricing (Commission 1976). A further proposal to harmonise the tax arrangements for the carry-over of losses was also issued (Commission, 1984).

There are therefore four issues in the taxation of companies that the Commission has tried to change. These are the harmonisation of the treatment of distributed profits, the taxable base, the tax rates, and the technical treatment of cross-border transactions.

The Treatment of Distributions

The simplest corporate tax system is the classical system,[5] used in Luxembourg, the Netherlands and the USA in which dividends are subject to income tax without any credit against corporate tax. One advantage of the system is its simplicity. A disadvantage is that in principle saving through the purchase of equity is discouraged, because of the 'double taxation' of dividends.

There are two types of system which reduce the extent of double taxation of dividends. One is simply to charge a lower rate of corporation tax on distributed profits than on undistributed profits. This 'split-rate' system is used in Germany, Japan and Portugal. The other system, which has become widespread in the last two decades, is the imputation system. Corporate tax is charged at one rate, regardless of the destination of profits, but if profits are distributed shareholders are given a tax credit which reduces their liability to personal tax. Thus part of the corporation tax is in effect treated as an advance payment of personal tax. The degree to which this reduces the double taxation of corporate income depends on the proportion of corporate tax which is imputed as personal income.

The Commission's 1975 proposals advocated use of the imputation system. The reasons for this choice were explicitly to encourage greater neutrality with regard to company finance, and with regard to the choice about whether to incorporate. Subsidiary reasons were to limit tax avoidance and to develop the share market.

One problem with an imputation system is the treatment of the personal tax-credit when the shareholder resides in a different country to the company distributing profits. For instance, if a Frenchman owns shares in a British company, should a tax credit be given to the Frenchman? If the answer is no, he is essentially facing a classical system and so there is discrimination against shareholders residing in a different country to that in which they invest.

To avoid this problem, in its 1975 proposals the Commission proposed that all shareholders living within the Community should benefit from the same amount of tax credit as that given to domestic residents. In other words, French shareholders in a British company would receive the same tax credit as equivalent British shareholders. This means that the French government would be giving credit for taxes paid in Britain, so the Commission proposed a clearing house to redistribute revenues from the country where corporate taxes were paid to that where the tax credit is redeemed.

The Tax Base

The Commission's proposal of 1975 was eventually referred back to it by the European Parliament because although it proposed a harmonised tax system and tax rates, it did not contain any proposals for harmonisation of the tax base. The Commission produced a 'preliminary draft' proposal in 1988. This closely follows the proposals of earlier directives concerning the calculation of commercial profits. It differs from current practice by some member states in various ways, including the treatment of stocks and of capital gains and losses. The most important changes are, however, those relating to the depreciation of assets for tax purposes.

The Commission is suggesting that the depreciation rates applied to assets for accounting purposes should be used for tax calculations. This is the system used in several European countries. It would, amongst other things, prevent accelerated depreciation, which has been used by some countries as a means of encouraging investment. If accounting depreciation rates are close to true economic depreciation rates and full allowance is given for the costs of finance, then the result would be a tax system approaching one type of neutrality, in that the pre-tax rate of return would approach the post-tax rate of return, and only economic rent would be taxed. However, companies generally prefer to apply higher depreciation rates than the true economic rate, in order to reduce the effective rate of tax. Some guidelines would be necessary. It is worth noting that where this 'at the company's discretion' principle is currently operated, typical depreciation rates differ between countries. This may be because there is a different composition of capital stocks between countries, so true depreciation rates actually are different. However, it may be that accounting practices are not uniform across the Community, in which case the Commission's proposals would not result in a standardisation of the tax base across Europe.

If the proposals were adopted, the assets which can be depreciated would change in some countries. All buildings would be depreciable — a change from current British and Irish practice which excludes commercial buildings. Research and development and start up costs would be depreciated over five years, as would goodwill. Other items of interest are that either straight line or declining balance (at three times the straight line rate) would be available, at the option of the firm. Pooling of assets for depreciation at some combined aggregate rate, as allowed in some member states, would be disallowed. There are no provisions for the indexation of depreciation allowances and replacement cost depreciation is rejected. Hence Denmark, for one, would be asked to drop its indexation of machinery depreciation. The result would be that inflation would increase the effective tax burden.

The other directive of note on the harmonisation of the tax base is a 1984 directive on the carry over of losses. This is more generous than almost any existing treatment, suggesting unlimited carry forward, and a two year period of carry back.

It is apparent, then, that the Commission has avoided some more radical changes which could be made to the calculation of the tax base. In particular are the cash-flow tax and the unitary tax.

The cash-flow corporation tax is really a type of classical tax system, in that it taxes corporate income and no credit is given to shareholders. In one form it involves the granting of 100 per cent allowances for all assets bought during a year, and the ending of interest deductibility. The simplest way of thinking of the economic effects of such a tax is that the government takes part ownership of companies. The advantage of such a system is that it is neutral with respect to domestic investment decisions, in that if a firm needs to provide a 5 per cent rate of return to its shareholders, the required pre-corporate tax rate of return which the firm needs to earn is 5 per cent — regardless of the tax rate. If the firm earns just enough to provide shareholders with a sufficient return, the tax paid will be zero; if a firm earns rent over and above what is required to satisfy shareholders the government will take a share. In addition, the tax system is perfectly neutral as regards the way in which firms raise finance.

Another possible tax base is a unitary one. This system is used by many of the states in the USA. Instead of taxing profits according to the place of production, or residence of the head office, unitary taxation involves application of some formula to total US profits, regardless of where they were made. The formula generally makes use of the percentage of total US work force in the particular state, percentage of total property in the state, and the percentage of sales.[6] If applied in Europe, it would mean that a company could manufacture solely in Italy, but if it sold through branches located throughout Europe, each member state could extract some tax (although given the property and payroll provisions, Italy would have the largest tax base).

The major advantage of the system is that it prevents the artificial transfer of profits from high tax to low tax countries, because of its *unitary* element. Suppose that a company operated in a high tax country. It could set up a sister company in a low tax country, and sell all its output to this company at a price which just eliminated all profits in the manufacturing country. The foreign subsidiary would sell the goods at the true price back to the manufacturing country (or anywhere else, for that matter) and so all profits would be earned in the low tax country. To prevent this, 'transfer pricing' rules have been made, in an attempt to ensure trade between companies under common ownership is at 'fair' prices and so profits are allocated to the country in which they are truly generated.[7] A unitary tax system would simply lump all related concerns into a single entity for tax purposes, so just because profits were formally declared in a low tax country would not prevent the manufacturing country taxing the profits. There would be no such entity as 'Ford of Spain', or 'Ford UK', at least for tax purposes. There would simply be 'Ford of Europe' (see McClure, 1989, for a more detailed discussion of unitary taxation).

Transfer pricing is not the only technical problem that might be removed by unitary taxation. Another is thin capitalisation. This problem occurs when there is a tax incentive for a company to finance investments abroad through debt rather than equity. For instance, a company may prefer to be financed by loans because the interest payments on the loans are tax-deductible. Of course, if the situation is one of a parent financing a subsidiary, it is not sufficient merely that the subsidiary is able to deduct interest payments for thin capitalisation to occur — the parent will be taxed on the interest it receives, and so if it faces the same tax rate as the subsidiary, there would be no gain. If the parent faces a lower tax rate, then there is a gain which companies might try to exploit. The result of thin capitalisation is a lower total tax burden.

The OECD has recently discussed this problem (OECD, 1988b) and suggested that there are two possible solutions. One is a fixed debt/equity ratio for all projects within a country — the problem being the defining of an acceptable ratio. The other (preferred) alternative is an arms length principle, interfering only when abuses are obvious. Obviously, a unitary tax would remove the problem as far as intra-group relations were concerned — the tax base would be the total group profits, regardless of where they were made.[8]

Unitary taxation therefore overcomes the problem of thin capitalisation and transfer pricing (provided that there is some agreement as to what constitutes related companies which should be taxed as a single unit). As long as there were some agreement on the base in calculating formulas, there is no reason why European member states should find the principle of unitary taxation distasteful. However, unitary tax base would not necessarily improve capital import or export neutrality. If a member state had particularly high tax rates, then there would be incentive to locate production elsewhere, and to export to that country, subjecting total profits only to the sales part of the formula, not the payroll or property parts. Only if tax rates were harmonised as well would true neutrality be achieved.

Foreign Source Income

The two key conditions for the achievement of neutrality in the international tax system are that a particular company faces the same tax rate, wherever it invests, and that competing companies face the same effective tax rate wherever they are established. Achieving these is likely to be difficult because they imply that the tax base and tax rates may need to be rather closer to each other than they currently are. However, some aspects of the international tax system seem specifically designed to achieve non-neutrality in the tax system.

Withholding taxes are a particular instance. All European countries charge corporation tax at a standard rate on all operations in their country, regardless of who owns the company. However, many also charge a withholding tax on all dividends or interest payments distributed to a shareholder or parent company resident in a foreign country. Withholding taxes are incompatible with capital import neutrality.

The other aspect of the international treatment of foreign source income is the treatment by the residence country of foreign source income. Two main systems are in use. One is to exempt all the profits earned abroad. Therefore tax is only paid in the source country. If all countries operated an exemption system, and no location specific rent was attributable to production, CIN would be attained.

The other system (the one used by Britain) is a credit system. The tax paid in the source country is compared with the tax that would have been paid had the rent been earned in the residence country. If the tax paid is less than that which would have been paid, the difference is paid by the parent to the residence country government; otherwise, no further action is taken. The economic effects clearly depend on the rate of tax in the residence country. Where the domestic tax rate is lower than that in all foreign countries, the system is just like an exemption system. Were the tax rate higher than the other countries, this rate would be paid wherever an investment was located and in that case CEN would be achieved. Mid-range tax rates would lead to mixed effects.

Technical Aspects

There have been very few mergers between European firms of equal size from different countries. There are good reasons to think that this may have been because of the tax system. Before looking at the technical aspects of the tax treatment of mergers, it is necessary to consider whether this is a problem at all.

Economists tend not to be as enthusiastic about mergers as company managers. One reason for merging is to reduce competition and increase market power, allowing the charging of higher prices and the generating of greater profits — at the consumers' expense. Such mergers are economically inefficient — a welfare loss results. Some, however, are not — when there are economies of scale, or the opening up of new avenues of arbitrage. Much of the Cecchini report (1988) on the costs of non-Europe focuses on the failure to exploit potential economies of scale in the European Community. For example, it estimates that the number of boiler makers in the EC would fall from 15 to 4 if government procurement were liberalised; there would be just 3 or 4 electric locomotive manufacturers compared with the current 16, if all economies of scale were to be fully realised. The most politically cautious way to achieve such rationalisation is by merging; simple competitive pressure may not be enough to overcome domestic political sentiment.

The tax problem of mergers arises from the treatment of foreign source income in imputation systems. When companies distribute profits to shareholders in an imputation system, they pre-pay a certain amount of income tax due on the dividends (the British-type ACT system), or else attach a tax credit to the dividend (the French-type avoir fiscal system). In an ACT system, the total paid like this can then be deducted from the corporation tax. The system works well as long as the income tax component is less than the total corporation tax. However, if most of a firm's profits are earned abroad, the domestic corporation tax charge may be small. The ACT is paid on all distributed profits, whatever their source. Thus it is possible that a firm which generates many of its profits abroad will pay more ACT on its distributions to its shareholders than it is liable to pay in corporation tax. Readers of the British financial press will recognise this problem as an example of unrelieved ACT.

The problem with mergers is therefore apparent — if two firms of equal profitability merge, they can only pay out final dividends from one country; they must pay ACT to that country; they can only offset this against the corporation tax due to that country. Merging two companies, both of which generated a certain amount of their profits abroad can therefore often lead to a larger tax bill (Chown, 1989). One way to cope with this problem is to take *all* taxes paid in the EC into account, refunding tax when the advance payment of income tax exceeds the domestic corporate tax liability, and using a clearing house system to refund the revenue authorities which had to make such payments out of the corporate taxes paid elsewhere in the Community. This problem is, of course, specific to imputation systems.

In January 1969 the Commission published a draft directive concerning tax and mergers (Commission, 1969a), together with a proposal on the relationship between parents and subsidiaries (Commission, 1969b). Together with a third draft directive on an arbitration procedure concerning disputes about transfer pricing (Commission, 1976), these directives form a package which the Commission and the European Employers Federation (UNICE) are pushing to get adopted in the next few years. These would *not* remove the tax problem with mergers — instead the aim is to remove some other, even more technical problems, such as roll over relief for losses in mergers, and the application of withholding taxes between parents and subsidiaries.

A proposal by the Commission which might seem to be of relevance as regards mergers and technical aspects of transnational operations is the European Company Statute (Commission, 1989). The Commission proposes to create a new legal entity called a European company. This, it is hoped, will facilitate trans-border co-operation and merger. In fact, although currently purely *legal* problems may complicate such activity, such difficulties can usually be overcome. A European company will have to operate under the same rules regarding *tax* as any other company, with one exception: that losses made by a subsidiary may be offset against a parent's profits. However, this is but a slight gain — losses made by foreign branches can be already be offset against a UK parent's profits, so companies generally set up new operations as branches and incorporate them as subsidiaries when profits are being made.

1.3 Prospects for Corporate Tax Harmonisation

The liturgy of the 1992 programmes is now a familiar one — the creation of a single European market of 320 million consumers, with a GDP of over £2500 billion (ECU 3800 billion, 1986 prices); a market where selling goods from Aberdeen to Athens is no more difficult than from Boston to Los Angeles; and where a company is not favoured by customers solely because it is Danish rather than Dutch. If the rhetoric is familiar, then so are the claimed benefits — greater competition, cheaper prices, more output, employment and wealth.

Little of the 1992 programme is related to corporation tax.[9] However, if all other differences between countries *other* than corporate tax differences are removed, then companies will be far more likely to take account of them. If a company knows that it need not be based in or to produce in Germany in order to persuade German consumers that its products are worth buying, then it will be more likely to be attracted to low tax countries. Already articles have appeared in the British press pointing out that 'a lack of uniformity [in corporate taxes] after 1992 offers companies great opportunities' ('chaos more likely than harmony', *Financial Times*, 13.3.1989). If companies do increase their tax 'planning' and start to change their decisions solely to take advantage of tax differences, it seems likely that the losers in this process — the revenue authorities of 'high' tax countries — will reduce their taxes. Harmonisation towards the lowest level of tax may occur, without any agreement on what a 'good' European corporate tax system should look like.

However, if the 1992 programme increases the importance of corporate taxes, it also may make agreement on the adoption of a harmonised system more difficult. The Single European Act left tax matters to be decided with unanimity. Any member of the European Community can veto any tax proposal (other issues can be decided with majority voting). In addition the Commission has decided that indirect taxes (VAT, excise duties) must be harmonised for the Internal Market to be completed.

The Commission's proposals for indirect taxes have been extensively examined elsewhere (e.g Lee, Pearson and Smith, 1988; Pearson and Smith, 1988). Indirect taxes do not generally distort competition. They are paid at the rate of tax prevalent in that country where final consumption takes place. Producing in a low tax country does not give a competitive advantage, because taxes are determined not by production or residence location, but by consumption location. The Commission bases its case for the harmonisation of indirect taxes not on direct efficiency arguments, but on reducing administrative burdens on cross-border trade.

There are two ways in which the harmonisation of indirect taxes might affect the possibility of getting an agreement to harmonise corporate taxes. One is that member states will have difficulty refusing the argument in favour of harmonising corporate taxes given that they have 'given in' once already. The other is that each successive attempt to harmonise a tax will be resisted more than the previous one because governments' freedom to manage their economies has already been reduced by previous harmonisations. Whatever the political problems, it is clear that harmonisation of corporate taxation is unlikely to have as serious consequences for budgetary revenue as indirect tax harmonisation, since on average corporate taxes account for less than a quarter of the revenue of indirect taxes — 7.2 per cent of total tax revenue in 1986, compared to 30.9 per cent raised by VAT and excise duties (OECD, 1988a). In the UK, the figures were 10.3 per cent and 29.2 per cent. (Only Luxembourg raised a higher proportion of its revenue from corporate taxes.)

Of course, objections to the harmonisation of corporate taxation are not solely political. There are economic arguments in favour of tax diversity. Insofar as governments adequately reflect the wishes of their electorate, different tax rates are desirable. Citizens of one country may wish for more public goods than another, so at least one rate of tax must differ. The efficiency case for uniformity of tax rates must be stronger than the benefits from allowing unrestrained 'consumer choice'. Another argument is that monetary union, if achieved, would severely restrict member states' monetary policy. As much freedom to change a country's fiscal stance as possible should therefore be left to its economic managers.[10]

However, it is clear that even these economic arguments carry less weight as far as corporate taxes are concerned than they might do with other taxes. As already noted, corporate taxes are not an important revenue source for most member states, so any lost revenue could be made up by other tax changes. In addition, given that capital is quite mobile, efficiency gains following corporate tax harmonisation may be quite large (whereas the immobility of labour implies that harmonisation of taxes on wages is unnecessary).

Nevertheless, on both economic and political grounds, it is clearly preferable to achieve a certain degree of capital import and export neutrality whilst allowing member states as much freedom as possible to set their own tax rates, rather than achieving the same impact through a rigid setting of tax rates.

1.4 Conclusions

This chapter has discussed three issues. First, it considered the case for harmonisation. It showed that the central issue is not whether the distribution of corporate taxes is fair, but whether unharmonised corporate taxes damage the efficiency of investment decisions. Decisions about where to invest and who invests can be influenced by corporate taxation. Ideally, there would be both capital export neutrality (CEN) and capital import neutrality (CIN).

Whether there is an efficiency loss caused by the absence of CEN or CIN depends on whether tax is on a source or a residence basis, and whether location specific rents are due to production having to be in a specific area, or whether they are due to the residence of the parent.

The second issue was to discuss the actual proposals of the European Commission, together with the problems which they raised. Proposals have been made to harmonise rates, base, system and some technical aspects of the European corporate tax system, but little progress has been made, and little sign of any willingness on the part of member states to agree a common European tax system has been evident. However, since the early 1970s there has been a certain degree of unilateral movement of member states towards an imputation system with a broad base and low rates — most recently evidenced by changes in the UK and the Netherlands, and the proposed German tax reform.

The final issue considered was the influence of the Single European Act and the completion of the internal market on the prospects of corporate tax harmonisation. It was argued that the removal of all other barriers to trade within the Community would lead to continued differences in corporate taxes having a more pervasive impact than is currently the case. Unanimity is still required for tax matters in the Council of Ministers.

The following chapter describes the current situation in more detail, giving the extent of non-neutralities in the current tax system. It also decomposes the *causes* of these non-neutralities. The third chapter presents evidence on the extent to which the current tax system distorts business decisions. The final chapter discusses the possible movement towards a European tax system which imposes smaller costs on the European economy.

NOTES

1. 'Corporate tax' here refers to the tax on income from capital.
2. Given the substantial change in taxation in the UK since 1984, this factor is clearly no bar to action if the political will is there.
3. It is interesting to note that the Inland Revenue could in theory, if not in law, take identical action even if Coca-Cola sold its cans via Sainsbury's. Since it would be taxed on deemed profits of 30p a can, Sainsbury's would only sell cans if it could buy them for 10p each. At this price, Coca-Cola would just be willing to accept.
4. To convince the Inland Revenue that a company has central management and control in another country it is necessary to show that most if not all directors live in that country, and that board meetings take place there, amongst several other requirements.
5. The classification used in this section between classical, imputation and split-rate systems is conventional when discussing this issue. There are not, however, clear-cut differences between the systems — the split-rate can be analytically identical to the imputation system and the two are combined by Germany which has a split-rate system but imputes *all* the tax paid on distributed profits to personal income tax.
6. Unitary taxation has acquired a poor reputation among European businesses, because it is associated with the Californian unitary tax. California applied the unitary principle to *worldwide* profits made by any firm operating in that state. Generally, when the term 'unitary taxation' is used in this report, it is referring to a European unitary tax — a tax on all profits made in Europe, not worldwide profits.
7. In the UK the transfer pricing rules have not proved to be particularly burdensome. Most transfer pricing is done for companies by advisers who will advise on the minimum defensible approach to avoid objections by the Inland Revenue.
8. Whatever European solutions to these problems are found, it is likely that thin capitalisation and transfer pricing abuses could continue through non-EC third parties.
9. There is a draft directive on the treatment of cross border mergers amongst the 300 directives which the Commission wishes to be adoped by the end of 1992.
10. A fuller summary of the case for tax diversity is given in Cnossen (1989).

CHAPTER 2

THE CURRENT EUROPEAN TAX SYSTEM

How can you compare the burden of taxation on business in different countries? It clearly is insufficient to merely look at the 'headline' tax rate — 35 per cent in the UK, 56 per cent in West Germany etc. This is because the tax *base* and tax *treatment of dividends* are very different in each country. For instance, in the UK, the capital allowance rate on plant and machinery is 25 per cent reducing balance, and in West Germany typically 10 per cent. It can be argued that the UK's corporation tax rate on distributed profits is not 35 per cent, but 10 per cent, because 25 per cent of the tax is advanced payment of individual's personal income tax.

Economists have developed measures of the *effective marginal* tax rate which take all these factors into account (King and Fullerton, 1984). The basic principle is simple. Suppose that, in the absence of taxes, companies need to provide their shareholders with a return of, say, 5 per cent. When a corporation tax is introduced, what rate of return would they need to earn before tax in order to continue to provide their shareholders with a 5 per cent return? It is the percentage difference between the pre-tax and post-tax rates of return which is known as the effective marginal tax rate. The King-Fullerton framework calculates this tax rate for a project which is 'marginal' in the absence of tax (i.e. one which just earns the required rate of return). It can therefore show whether a tax system is neutral in the sense of neither discouraging projects which would go ahead in the absence of tax, nor encouraging projects which would not go ahead in the absence of tax. The former would happen if the effective marginal tax rate were positive, the latter if it were negative; both distortions are found in Europe. In addition, by comparing the tax rates on different types of investment within a country, possibly financed from different sources, they can show whether the tax system is leading to a misallocation of resources, in that the tax system favours some investments over others.

These non-neutralities are distinct from those non-neutralities referred to in Chapter 1, although the general principles are much the same. There it was argued that projects may take place in the 'wrong' country, or be undertaken by the 'wrong' company, because of the tax system. This is possible because of non-neutralities affecting the marginal investment, but also because the average tax rates on economic rents (as described in the previous chapter, rent is the profit earned over and above the minimum necessary for the project to go ahead) differ across countries according to both the source country (where an investment takes place) and the residence country (the nationality of the parent company).

This chapter therefore extends the standard King-Fullerton methodology in two ways. First, instead of looking at investments in a particular country by companies resident in that country, the model looks at investments by companies resident in the European Community when they invest in each of the other member states. As a consequence, the King-Fullerton effective marginal tax rate on an investment by a British company in France is compared to the tax rate on an identical investment by the same company in Germany or in any of the other countries covered by the analysis. The dispersion of these tax rates gives some indication of the degree of capital export *non*-neutrality[1] in each of the fourteen countries. An average of these dispersions gives a summary figure. Similarly, a measure of the degree of capital import non-neutrality can be found. Various reforms to the international tax system can be compared as to their impact in reducing the distortions found in the current system.

In addition to extending the King-Fullerton methodology to cover transnational investment, this chapter also develops it further in order to calculate the average tax rates on economic rent. Many investment projects are not marginal in the sense that they may or may not be undertaken; instead the issue is *where* they are located, and *who* invests.

Before describing the model, the tax systems currently in place in the EC are described.

2.1 The Current Situation

National Tax Rates

The tax rates applied by European governments together with those of Japan and the USA are given in Table 2.1. Some countries also have local corporate taxes, which vary from region to region. A typical rate is given in the table.

Table 2.1 also indicates the tax system in use. As described in Chapter 1, these different systems affect the rate of return received by shareholders on equity investment. As can seen from the table, there is a wide variation — in national tax rates, ranging from 10 per cent in Ireland (until the end of the century), to 56 per cent on

TABLE 2.1

National Tax Rates

	National Tax Rate	Type of Tax System	Local Taxes[1]	Imputation Rate[2]
Belgium	43	Imputation		33.3
Denmark	50	Imputation		20
France	42	Imputation		33.3
Germany	36/56	Split Rate/ Imputation	15	36
Greece	44	Imputation		44
Ireland	10[3]	Imputation		5.3
Italy	36	Imputation	16.2	36
Luxembourg	36 + 0.72[4]	Classical	6	–
Netherlands	35	Classical		–
Portugal	35/47	Split Rate		–
Spain	35	Imputation		9.1
UK	35	Imputation		25
Japan	32/42	Split rate	12	–
USA	34	Classical	3.5	–

Source: OECD (1989).

Notes: [1] Typical rates: German and Italian are tax deductible, whereas the rates given here for Japan, America and Luxembourg are net.
[2] Percentage of gross dividend.
[3] Until 31.12.2000, for manufacturing companies only. Under bilateral treaties, other countries sometimes assume that a higher rate of tax has been paid by companies investing in Ireland.
[4] 2% levy (deductible) for the Unemployment fund.

undistributed profits in Germany. Most European countries now operate an imputation system.

The Treatment of Foreign Source Income

National tax rates only determine the final tax rate when the source country (the country where investment takes place) is the same as the country of residence (the country where the parent is based). Otherwise, the overall tax rate can be changed by the tax treatment of foreign source income.

Many countries levy withholding taxes on profits as they are transferred from the source country to the parent. These withholding taxes often vary according to whether profits are transferred as interest payments or as dividend payments. The withholding tax on dividends also often differs with the degree of ownership of the subsidiary by the parent — generally, the larger the proportion of the subsidiary owned by a shareholder (in this case, the parent company), the lower the withholding tax rate. The withholding tax rates on dividend payments from a subsidiary wholly owned by the parent are given in Table 2.2.

TABLE 2.2

Withholding Tax Rates[1]

Source	Residence													
	B	Dk	F	WG	G	Ire	I	Lux	Nl	P	S	UK	Jap	USA
B		15	15	15	15	15	15	15	15	15	15	15	15	15
Dk	15		0	10	30	0	15	5	0	10	10	0	10	5
F	10	0		0	25	10	15	5	5	15	10	5	10	5
WG	25	25	25		25	20	25	25	25	15	25	20	15	15
G	25	42	42	25		42	25	42	35	42	42	42	42	42
Ire	0	0	0	0	0		0	0	0	0	0	0	0	0
I	15	15	15	32	25	15		15	0	15	15	5	10	5
Lux	10	5	5	10	15	5	15		3	15	5	5	15	5
Nl	5	0	15	10	5	0	0	3		25	5	5	5	5
P	12	10	12	12	12	12	12	12	12		10	10	12	12
S	15	10	10	10 ·	20	20	15	10	10	10		10	10	20
UK	0²	0²	0	0	0	0	0	0²	0²	0	0		0	0²
Jap	15	10	10	10	20	10	10	20	10	20	10	10		10
USA	15	5	5	15	30	5	10	5	5	30	30	5	10	

Source: Price Waterhouse (1988).
Notes: [1] Based on repatriation of dividends to a parent owning 100% of the subsidiary. Withholding taxes are often higher when a lower proportion of the subsidiary is owned by the shareholder.
[2] Half tax credit to non-resident companies possessing 10% or more of the company, subject to a 5% withholding tax on the gross payment. In other words, the shareholder is entitled to a refund of some of the ACT which a company must pay on the full valueof its distribution, even though some shareholders are foreign and are therefore unable to claim the tax benefit.

Foreign source income may be taxed yet a third time. After corporation tax in the country of source, and any withholding tax, there may be a further tax liability in the country of residence. This is not always the case, as many countries simply exempt all foreign source income. However, some, including the UK, operate a credit system. In these countries, revenue authorities compare the tax *actually* paid abroad on the repatriated dividends with the tax that would have been charged had the profits been generated domestically. If domestic tax would have been higher, then the difference between this and the tax paid abroad is paid by the parent company to the country of residence.[2] The position is shown in Table 2.3.

TABLE 2.3

Treatment of Foreign Source Income

Treatment	Dividends Repatriated to:
Credit:	Greece, Portugal, Spain, UK, Japan, USA.
Exemption:	Belgium[1], France[1], Germany, Ireland, Italy[1], Luxembourg, the Netherlands.
Mixed:	Denmark (Exemption if from France, Germany, Ireland, Portugal or Spain; Credit otherwise).

Source: Price Waterhouse (1988).

Note: [1] A proportion is not exempt.

Apart from the credit and exemption systems, there is a third way of treating foreign source income. This is to exempt a proportion of it, but to charge domestic corporation tax on the remainder. This system is used in Belgium, France and Italy, which respectively exempt 95 per cent, 90 per cent and 60 per cent of foreign source income.

The Tax Base

Companies may deduct from their profits the amount by which their assets depreciate. However, tax authorities cannot be expected to know the true economic depreciation rate for each item of machinery. Two strategies are available to revenue authorities. One is to operate on a hands-off basis and let companies use accounting definitions of depreciation for tax purposes. The other is to specify depreciation rates for tax purposes for particular categories of goods. Both strategies are used in Europe — France using the former, for example, and the UK using the latter. But it is important to note that use of accounting definitions does not mean that the true economic depreciation rates are in use. Casual inspection of 'typical' depreciation rates in the countries permitting companies to choose their own shows that they differ substantially. This might simply reflect different composition of assets (France may have a lower typical depreciation rate for plant and machinery than Belgium

41

because it tends to invest in longer lasting assets). More likely, accounting norms and practices differ.

Table 2.4 gives typical depreciation rates for tax purposes in the European Community, Japan and the USA. In the analysis, assumptions about the true economic depreciation rates also need to be made.

TABLE 2.4

Typical Depreciation Rates (straight line unless otherwise noted)

	Plant and Machinery	Industrial Buildings	Commercial Buildings
Belgium	20	5	3
Denmark	25% (declining balance) in first year then 30% (inflation adjusted)	6% for ten years then 2%	–
France	15	5	5
Germany	10	2	4
Greece	15	8	5
Ireland	75% (declining balance) in first year then 25%	50% in first year then 4%	–
Italy	15	15% for three years then 3%	15% for three years then 3%
Luxembourg	20	4	2
Netherlands	10	3	3
Portugal	15	4	2
Spain	10	3	3
UK	25% (declining balance)	4	–
Japan	10	2.2	1.5
USA	28.6% declining balance for three years, then 14.3% straight line	3.2	3.2

Source: OECD (1989), IBFD (1988), Coopers and Lybrand (1988), Touche Ross International (1989).

Finally, most countries base the depreciation allowance on historic cost value. In other words, if a company bought a good in 1980 which could be depreciated at a rate of 10 per cent of the original value for 10 years, then in 1989 the company will be able to deduct exactly the same amount in money terms from profits as it deducted in 1980, despite the fact that inflation will have eroded the value of this deduction. Inflation rates vary throughout Europe, and so the erosion of the value of the depreciation allowance will take place at different rates. Therefore even with identical tax systems, the effective marginal tax burden on companies will differ because of inflation. When there is inflation, the relative burden of taxation between companies operating in different countries may change — just because the UK has a more generous tax system than Spain in the absence of inflation does not necessarily mean that this will be the case if inflation in both countries is 10 per cent.

Grants

The tax system is not the only way in which government actions can distort company decisions about where to invest. All European governments give special incentives to companies to invest either in particular regions of their countries or, in several cases, simply to invest anywhere in their country. These regional incentives take many forms. The model specified below takes account of the vast majority of them, by dividing them into three common groups — grants, special depreciation allowances, and soft loans. Often the coverage and value of these regional incentives varies according to the precise region in which an investment takes place. For instance, the subsidies given to investments in Sicily and Northern Ireland are higher than those given to most of Umbria and Tyneside, but even these areas are favoured over Milan and London, which receive no special treatment outside of the standard tax system.

If governments were not restrained, it is easy to envisage that a competition to attract foreign investment would develop within the European Community. In addition, domestic companies under pressure from competition from elsewhere in the Community might be given privileged tax treatment. Capital import and export neutralities would be sacrificed inasmuch as some countries did not 'keep up' with the others, and the costs of attracting investors would spiral. Recognising this, the Commission has imposed a series of conditions which must be met before investment in a region can be given the benefit of a regional incentives (Commission, 1988b). These conditions include the unemployment rate being very high compared with the EC average, or relatively high compared with the national average, and similar conditions related to a region's average income per head. Limits are also placed on the total proportion of the costs of an investment which can be met by government subsidies.[3]

2.2 The Model of Transnational Tax Rates

The model used to derive the results given in this chapter is described in detail in Crooks, Devereux, Pearson and Wookey (1989) and only its broad outline is summarised here. It is assumed that a company must earn 5 per cent after tax on a project to satisfy the providers of capital. Initially it is assumed that no rent is earned (in other words, the rate of return on the projects in the absence of tax is 5 per cent), so the minimum necessary profit is being made by the company. It is assumed that investment in foreign countries is undertaken by wholly-owned subsidiaries, financed solely by equity from the parent.[4] Some of the costs of a project can be written off in the form of depreciation allowances as given by the source country. As some of these allowances are granted in the future, they must be discounted at the company's discount rate. Post-tax profits made by the subsidiary are repatriated to the parent in the form of dividends. The parent raises finance domestically, through debt, retentions or new equity.

As in the King-Fullerton study, the company's discount rate depends on how the parent raises funding. If debt finance is used, all of the costs of servicing the debt (in this case interest payments) are tax deductible, thereby reducing the company's discount rate. The servicing of funds raised from new equity issues is assumed to be through dividend payments. Under a 'classical' system, no relief is given for dividends and so the discount rate is simply taken to be the market interest rate. Under an imputation system, however, relief is given, which reduces the discount rate. The tax credit available under the imputation system is therefore taken into account. However, in the results shown below the position is simplified by setting income tax rates and capital gains tax rates to zero (as would be the case in the UK for a pension fund, for example). Zero-rated income tax payers are assumed to qualify for a tax rebate equal to the tax credit under the imputation system. The third way of raising funds is from retained earnings. Corporate tax will be charged on the retained earnings, as will capital gains tax when the increase in share values is realised. In principle, then, the discount rate will depend on the relative size of the tax rates on income and capital gains. However, since these tax rates are assumed to be zero in deriving the results given below, the discount rate on retained earnings is simply the market interest rate.

The other relevant piece of information used in the model is the real depreciation rates. It is assumed that these are 12.25 per cent for plant and machinery, 2.5 per cent for commercial buildings, and 3.6 per cent for industrial buildings, throughout Europe. The accuracy of these rates is not crucial for the purpose of this report — the principal aim is not to provide exact measures of effective marginal tax rates, but to see by how much countries differ in their treatment of an identical investment.

This model allows for a 14x14 matrix of effective marginal tax rates to be calculated for nine investment projects: the combination of three types of finance — debt, equity and retained earnings — and three types of asset — plant and machinery, industrial building and commercial buildings. In order to reduce the amount of information to more easily assimilated proportions, a weighted average of these projects is used. The weights used — 50 per cent plant and machinery, 15 per cent commercial buildings, 35 per cent industrial buildings, and 70 per cent retained earnings, 25 per cent debt, 5 per cent new equity — are intended to roughly correspond to an average of actual investments made in Europe (Crooks et al., 1989).

In summary, the model works as follows:

(1)   The parent raises all the money for a project in the residence country, by retaining earnings from other projects, borrowing, or issuing new equity.

(2)   The investment is undertaken by a subsidiary in the source country (which in some cases will be the residence country of the parent); the subsidiary is wholly owned by the parent.

(3)   The subsidiary invests in plant and machinery, and industrial and commercial buildings.

(4)   Depreciation allowances and other allowable costs of the project are written off against profits in the source country. (It is assumed that taxable profits are always positive).

(5)   The source country taxes the profits.

(6)   All post-tax profits are remitted to the parent in the form of dividends.

(7)   The source country may impose an additional witholding tax on these dividends.

(8)   If the resident country operates a credit system it may impose a further tax on profits earned in countries with a lower tax rate.

As noted above, inflation can affect the size of the effective marginal tax rate. The model can calculate effective marginal tax rates at any inflation level; below, results are presented for two inflation rates, 0 and 10 per cent.

Finally, as the focus is not merely on marginal investments, average tax rates on projects earning rent are calculated. The average tax rate is defined simply as the proportion of economic rent taken in tax. Clearly, this concept cannot apply to an investment which does not earn an economic rent (pre-tax). We therefore need to distinguish effective marginal tax rates and effective average tax rates. The two are presented separately below, although they rely on the same set of assumptions as described above. Note that inflation can also affect the effective average tax rate.

2.3 Results from the Model

(a) Effective Marginal Tax Rates

What is the current situation?

The model contains fourteen countries, so there are 196 combinations of source and residence countries. Table 2.5 shows one set of the combinations; the pre-tax rates of return necessary in order to generate a post-tax rate of return of 5 per cent for an investment in an 'average' basket of assets (as defined above) weighted according to the importance of each type of finance. Hence no rent is being earned. Inflation is set at 0 per cent. The fact that some of these pre-tax rates of return are less than 5 per cent should be noted, indicating that (given our assumptions regarding the economic depreciation

TABLE 2.5

Weighted average of required pre-tax rates of return necessary to earn a 5% post-tax return

Investment in	Investment from													
	B	Dk	F	WG	G	Ire	I	Lux	Nl	P	S	UK	Jap	USA
B	5.83	6.34	6.53	6.36	6.36	7.17	7.24	6.56	6.71	6.71	6.66	6.61	6.78	6.66
Dk	8.35	7.02	7.24	7.64	9.36	7.84	9.42	7.53	7.38	8.01	7.96	7.28	7.83	7.63
F	6.26	5.67	5.75	5.69	6.75	6.81	7.09	6.03	6.17	6.59	6.32	6.08	6.68	6.12
WG	9.07	8.63	8.92	8.86	8.66	9.23	10.3	8.92	9.12	8.21	9.06	8.51	8.00	8.15
G	6.69	7.51	7.73	6.46	5.55	8.52	7.27	7.77	7.41	7.95	7.89	7.82	7.73	7.89
Ire	4.68	4.53	4.64	4.54	4.57	5.08	4.53	4.67	4.77	4.85	4.74	4.71	4.91	4.74
I	6.30	6.07	6.24	6.92	6.52	6.87	5.60	6.28	5.91	6.42	6.38	5.97	6.26	6.02
Lux	6.70	6.55	6.38	6.44	6.69	6.98	7.72	6.19	6.43	7.05	6.50	6.45	7.18	6.49
Nl	6.28	7.03	6.73	6.27	6.47	6.52	6.74	6.09	6.11	7.58	6.30	6.25	7.64	6.30
P	6.36	6.00	6.28	6.11	6.13	6.87	7.04	6.30	6.43	6.59	6.30	6.25	6.40	6.39
S	6.86	6.28	6.48	6.30	6.88	7.75	7.68	6.49	6.63	7.00	6.10	6.54	7.64	7.20
UK	5.71	7.24	6.11	5.91	6.64	6.60	6.93	5.63	5.75	7.02	6.20	6.12	7.83	6.35
Jap	8.38	7.59	7.85	7.61	8.43	8.55	9.08	8.68	8.01	8.87	7.96	7.90	8.24	7.96
USA	6.55	6.54	6.02	6.30	7.20	6.59	6.96	6.04	6.17	7.59	7.54	6.08	7.06	5.93

rate) some projects are effectively subsidised by the tax system. For the purposes of this report, however, what is rather more important is the distribution of returns.

A British parent, for example, deciding where to locate an investment, faces very different possible tax rates. If it invested in the UK it would need to earn 6.1 per cent pre-tax in order to be able to pay its shareholders 5 per cent post-tax. If it invested in a wholly-owned Irish subsidiary, it would need to earn only 4.7 per cent to be able to provide its shareholders with the same return. If it invested in Germany it would have to earn over 8 per cent. Clearly, this could drive the British investor away from Germany which, if production in Germany could be done at lower cost, would result in an overall welfare loss. There is no capital export neutrality between these fourteen countries.

Now consider an investment which has to be undertaken anywhere along the Mediterranean. Other things being equal, a British firm would need to earn a minimum of around 6 per cent and would invest in Italy. A French firm would need to earn a quarter of a per cent less, by investing in France. If, however, the project *had* to be located in Italy, it would be the British firm which had the slight advantage. In so far as there is this difference, the existence of any residence location specific rents would result in a loss of welfare caused by the absence of capital import neutrality. In general, looking along a row, the figures are much closer together than the figures down a column. This reflects the fact that the current transnational tax system is rather closer to being a source based system than a residence based one. For projects which must be located in a particular country, this implies that the current system is not particularly far away from capital import neutrality. However, if a project could be located anywhere in Europe, the variation in required tax rates is much higher.

A summary of Table 2.5 is given in Table 2.6. The first column gives the required rate of return were a company to invest in its home country. The second column gives the *average* rate of return that companies from the other countries included in the model would need to earn if they invested *in* that country. The third column gives the average rate of return companies *from* that country would need to earn, when they invest in the rest of the countries modelled.

The next two columns give the measures of the dispersion of tax rates that were the aim of this model. The standard deviation of investments *in* each country gives one indication of the degree of

TABLE 2.6

Required pre-tax rates of return

	Own Country	Investing in:	Investing from:	Standard Deviation in:	Standard Deviation from:	Ratio of Protection
BELGIUM	5.83	6.67	6.78	0.34	1.12	0.98
DENMARK	7.02	7.96	6.61	0.70	0.95	1.20
FRANCE	5.75	6.33	6.70	0.43	1.00	0.94
GERMANY	8.86	8.83	6.35	0.55	0.98	1.39
GREECE	5.55	7.59	6.97	0.73	1.20	1.09
IRELAND	5.08	4.68	7.41	0.15	1.02	0.63
ITALY	5.60	6.32	7.54	0.34	1.42	0.84
LUXEMBOURG	6.19	6.74	6.69	0.39	1.13	1.01
NETHERLANDS	6.11	6.63	6.68	0.49	1.03	0.99
PORTUGAL	6.59	6.37	7.22	0.27	0.95	0.88
SPAIN	6.10	6.90	6.91	0.53	1.05	1.00
UK	6.12	6.46	6.65	0.62	0.94	0.97
JAPAN	8.24	8.22	7.07	0.44	0.86	1.16
USA	5.93	6.67	6.76	0.55	0.92	0.99
Average of column	6.35	6.88	6.88	0.47	1.04	1.01

capital import non-neutrality for those goods which are not tradable — for instance, bridges. The standard deviation 'from' is a more general summary measure of the degree of capital export non-neutrality faced by a company from that country.

The final column is not directly related to capital import/export neutrality. It is the average rate of return required when investing in a country divided by the average required rate of return when investing from that country. The purpose of this measure is to try to give some indication of the direction in which the international tax system is encouraging capital to flow. If the measure is less than 1, then it is cheaper for companies from other countries to invest in that country, than for companies based in that country to invest abroad. Therefore, other things being equal, international capital is likely to flow into the country. Of course, in fact other things are not equal; any inflow of capital would have repercussions on the exchange rate and numerous other economic variables. However, some of the ratios are of interest. Ireland is the most extreme case, being on average the cheapest place to invest in, and most expensive place to invest from — clear evidence of the size of the well-documented efforts to increase investment in Ireland. In contrast, it seems that the tax systems of both Germany and Japan encourage investment abroad rather than foreign investment in their domestic economy. This is perhaps as would be hoped, given their large surpluses on their trade accounts — some offsetting net flows on the capital account are desirable.

The results in Table 2.6 clearly show that differences in countries' treatment of corporate income could distort the decisions by companies about where to invest and discriminate against companies resident in some countries rather than others. This is insufficient to prove that there is a problem. It may be that despite the size of the differences in tax rates, they are not large enough to lead companies to change their behaviour, or perhaps companies only rarely feel that there is a choice about where to invest, or about who should invest in a particular project. This issue — whether different tax rates matter *in practice* — is returned to in the next chapter. In the rest of this chapter, the specific features which cause non-neutralities in the tax system are identified.

What causes non-neutrality?

It would, perhaps, be constructive if these results were decomposed, in order to identify just what causes the capital export and import non-neutralities. For example, the importance of tax *rates* is far greater when finance is provided by debt than when it is provided by equity. The reason is because tax rates matter twice for debt. The tax rate of the source country is applied to profits regardless of the nature of any finance. However, if finance is provided by the parent borrowing in the country of residence then the tax rate in the residence country will matter as well because it determines the value of debt interest being deductible from the corporate tax base.

Using the asset and finance weights given earlier, the current situation is summarised in column 1 of table 2.7. The figures are the standard deviation of the effective pre-tax rates of return required by a company from that country when investing in any one of the twelve European countries in the model (Japan and the USA are not considered in this exercise), in order to provide a 5 per cent post-tax return and so is a measure of the lack of capital export neutrality. Two figures are given, one for a zero inflation rate, and one for an inflation rate of 10 per cent. It is apparent, comparing the two columns, that inflation increases the dispersion of required pre-tax rates of return, or, equivalently, inflation increases the degree of capital export non-neutrality. The average of the standard deviations — a simple summary of the overall extent of non-neutrality in

TABLE 2.7

Decomposing the sources of non-neutrality in the international tax system: standard deviation of required rates of return for companies resident in each country

Inflation	(1) Current Situation (mid 1989)		(2) Common Tax Base		(3) Common National Tax Rate (50%)		(4) Current Systems (credit/ exemption)		(5) No Withholding Taxes Exemption System		(6) Credit System		(7) Harmonise Everything Except the Base (1975 proposal)	
	0	10	0	10	0	10	0	10	0	10	0	10	0	10
BELGIUM	1.11	1.54	0.79	1.36	0.95	1.39	0.65	0.82	0.61	0.77	0.49	0.55	0.51	0.66
DENMARK	0.99	1.56	0.85	1.46	0.84	1.50	0.75	1.01	0.60	0.76	0.51	0.66	0.51	0.66
FRANCE	1.01	1.66	0.93	1.59	0.90	1.59	0.63	0.80	0.61	0.77	0.49	0.54	0.51	0.66
GERMANY	1.01	1.56	0.84	1.46	0.48	0.89	1.01	1.48	1.01	1.48	0.84	1.15	0.51	0.66
GREECE	1.20	1.48	0.82	1.40	1.02	1.31	0.66	0.84	0.60	0.76	0.49	0.56	0.51	0.66
IRELAND	1.01	1.86	1.00	1.85	0.79	1.49	0.67	0.93	0.67	0.93	0.67	0.93	0.51	0.66
ITALY	1.44	1.99	1.00	1.71	1.39	2.03	0.94	1.20	0.60	0.76	0.50	0.59	0.51	0.66
LUXEMBOURG	1.05	1.73	0.97	1.69	0.86	1.56	0.62	0.80	0.62	0.80	0.50	0.57	0.51	0.66
NETHERLANDS	1.03	1.66	0.85	1.50	0.86	1.48	0.63	0.83	0.63	0.83	0.51	0.62	0.51	0.66
PORTUGAL	0.87	1.45	0.84	1.47	0.79	1.48	0.66	0.92	0.64	0.86	0.47	0.57	0.51	0.66
SPAIN	1.06	1.73	0.98	1.72	0.81	1.43	0.63	0.82	0.63	0.82	0.51	0.61	0.51	0.66
UK	0.93	1.58	0.90	1.58	0.76	1.41	0.62	0.81	0.62	0.81	0.50	0.60	0.51	0.66
CEN	1.06	1.65	0.90	1.57	0.87	1.46	0.71	0.94	0.65	0.86	0.54	0.66	0.51	0.66
CIN	1.10	1.77	0.93	1.68	0.95	1.55	0.75	1.10	0.69	1.06	0.69	1.02	0.51	0.66

Europe — increases by over 50 per cent as inflation rises by 10 per cent.

A figure for interpreting the degree of CIN is also given. This is the standard deviation of the matrix given in Table 2.5. The justification for this measure is that it is appropriate for a good that can be produced in any country, and exported to any other country. It too rises sharply as inflation increases.

Column 2 harmonises the tax base so that each country applies the same depreciation rates to assets: namely 20 per cent, 3 per cent and 5 per cent straight line for plant and machinery, commercial and industrial buildings respectively. There is a small fall in the average dispersion of tax rates when investing from a country, both in the no inflation case and when inflation is 10 per cent. Capital export neutrality is therefore promoted, as is capital import neutrality, although for both measures the improvement is not very great.

In column 3 all local taxes on corporate income are abolished, and the national tax rates are fixed at 50 per cent (this is rather higher than the current average but was chosen as it is the mid point of the 45–55 per cent tax rate range that the Commission suggested in its 1975 proposals). The tax bases are as under existing regimes, as are the tax systems (i.e. whether there is a classical, split-rate or imputation system). The dispersion in tax rates when investing from a country in this case falls by 18 per cent in the no-inflation case, and by under 12 per cent when inflation is 10 per cent. Similar falls occur in the dispersion of the matrix (the chosen indicator of the degree of capital import neutrality). The significance of this result is that harmonising tax rates does little to improve the position with regard to capital export and import neutrality, despite the fact that outliers are brought into line — for example, Ireland's tax rate is increased from 10 per cent. The reason for this counter-intuitive result is actually rather simple: generally, when governments are generous in their tax rates relative to the rest of the developed world, they tend to be less than generous with other aspects of the tax system; the permitted rates of depreciation, for example. Partial harmonisation — harmonising one aspect of the tax system — need not advance the cause of neutrality at all. Column 3 suggests that the radical and politically painful process of merely harmonising tax rates does little to improve neutrality in the allocation of resources in the European Community.

Withholding taxes on the payment of divdends abroad are abolished in column 4 while all other aspects of tax regimes are as they currently exist. The impact on both CEN and CIN as compared with the current situation (column 1) is much greater than that following the alignment of tax rates. Withholding taxes apparently account for a third or more of the variation in required pre-tax rates of return on marginal investments. This is not quite a change to totally source based taxation, however. Some countries have exemption systems for all foreign source income, and so there will be entirely source based taxation; however, where a credit system is in use (Denmark, Greece, Portugal, Spain, and the UK) there may still be an additional tax levied on profits earned abroad. In column 5, complete exemption of foreign source income is added. This results in a further modest improvement in capital export and import neutrality. (Note that for projects financed by retained earnings, under our assumptions, capital import neutrality for projects which must be located in a particular country would be achieved. However, more generally, this would not be the case.)

The results of abolishing all withholding taxes but switching to the credit system (column 6) rather than the exemption system would give a CEN measure of 0.54 in the absence of inflation, and 0.66 in the presence of 10 per cent inflation across the Community. These figures are somewhat superior to the results gained by harmonising to an exemption system. This, of course, is to be expected, since for the countries with very high domestic tax rates, capital export neutrality is virtually achieved — if companies invest in countries with lower tax rates, then they are charged the difference between these and the domestic tax rates on repatriation of profits. The CIN measures were almost identical to those obtained by an exemption system, at 0.69 and 1.02.

To some extent, this large improvement in neutrality reflects the fact that it is assumed that the special treatment of Ireland is discontinued. Under certain bilateral treaties, the 10 per cent tax rate imposed by Ireland is currently treated as being 43 per cent when calculating any additional tax upon repatriation of profits to non-Irish parent companies. Were Ireland to continue to benefit from this provision, there would be little improvement of neutrality by operating a credit system over and above the gain from abolishing withholding taxes. However, in column 6 it is assumed that other countries no longer offer this special treatment to Ireland and instead treat the tax rate as being 10 per cent. This gives a clearer indication of the position if normal credit systems were applied everywhere. It also permits direct comparison with column 7, in which the Irish tax rate is raised (with all other tax rates) to 50 per cent.

The final column gives the effect of adopting the Commission's 1975 proposals. In fact, it assumes harmonised tax rates at 50 per cent, an imputation system with a credit of 25 per cent of grossd dividends, and an exemption system. Only the base is left unharmonised. There is some improvement in CEN from column 5 although the improvement is, perhaps against expectations, rather small. Compared with simply abolishing withholding taxes and introducing a credit system everywhere, there is virtually no improvement in CEN.

Finally, the model was run with grants for all European Community countries. With measures of capital export non-neutrality of 1.92 and 3.17 for the zero and 10 per cent inflation cases respectively, and the corresponding CIN measures of 1.92 and 3.21, it is clear that, as would be expected and indeed intended, grants worsen the distortion about where to invest.

The fact that dispersion increases for investments in the different countries presumably illustrates that grants are an effective means of changing the incentives faced by companies when they make their investment decisions. However, they are a costly way of achieving this end — the *average* rate of return required when investing in the EC from another EC country and when inflation is 10 per cent falls by over four percentage points when grants are fully taken into account. In many countries, economically inefficient investment is being encouraged — indeed, in several regions the required real pre-tax rate of return can be *negative*, yet a post-tax rate of return of 5 per cent is generated. This does not necessarily make a case for the abolition of regional incentives. They are designed to attract investments which would not otherwise take place in that area, for social reasons. However, there may be still some competition between member states which wastefully pushes subsidies below what they need to be.

(b) Effective Average Tax Rates

Thus far, the analysis has focused on marginal investments. However, the location of projects which earn economic rent may also be distorted by the tax system. This section repeats the analysis done for marginal investments for those earning economic rent: profit over and above that which is necessary to satisfy the providers of capital for an investment.

Average tax rates on rent are not constant regardless of the amount of rent earned. The greater the rent, the less does the difference between the depreciation allowances allowed for in the tax system and the *true* economic depreciation rate matter. For instance, if a company earns a return of 100 per cent on its capital, the fact that it is only allowed to depreciate its plant and machinery over eight years when it actually lasts four years is much less likely to influence decisions than if the rate of return was 10 per cent.

As a consequence, the fact that a country has a lower than normal average tax rate on rent when rents are low does not mean that this is the case when rents are high. For instance, consider Figure 1.

FIGURE 1:

Average tax rate on rents earned by a British company investing in various European countries (equity financed, no inflation)

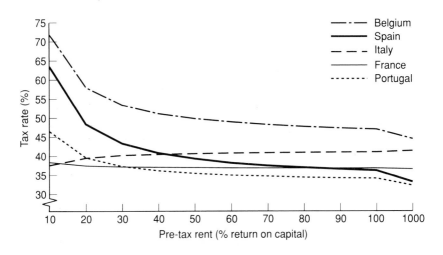

This shows the average tax rates on rent for a British company which is considering in which of five EC countries it might locate an investment. The investment reflects the weighted average of assets as described above. It must be financed by a new equity issue by the parent. There is no inflation. As the amount of rent earned increases, the average tax rate faced by the company changes.

Suppose that the company is able to locate the investment in any one of the five countries and that no country has a production location specific rent in excess of that of any other country. Clearly, whatever rent is earned, Belgium is rejected as an investment location, as it always has the highest average tax rate on rent. However, where the firm should rationally choose to locate depends on the expected amount of rent which will be earned. If the rent is around 10 per cent, Italy has the lowest rate of tax. With a rent of between 15 to 30 per cent, France would become the most favoured location. With rents above 30 per cent, Portugal has the lowest tax rate, and Italy, which had the lowest rate of tax on low rents, has the second highest tax rate.

Of course, if there really were no difference in the pre-tax rents that could be earned in each country, the different tax rates would result in no welfare loss. Relaxing this assumption, it is possible to see how European efficiency may be impared. For instance, if a pre-tax rent of 60 per cent could be earned in Belgium, the post-tax rent kept by the firm would be 30 per cent. If in Portugal, only 50 per cent rent might be earned pre-tax, but at an average tax rate on rent of about 35 per cent, the firm would keep 32.5 per cent. The rational firm would therefore locate in Portugal, despite the fact that the cost of producing there is greater than in Belgium.

The average tax rates clearly tend towards some level as the rent earned rises. As described elsewhere (Crooks *et al.*, 1989) the average tax rate is determined by three elements — the headline tax rate, the value of any depreciation allowances, and a term relating to the cost of finance. As rents get larger, the significance of the second term falls, leaving the average tax rate on very profitable investments as the headline tax rate plus or minus a cost of finance term. Hence Britain — with a low headline tax rate and comparatively low allowances — becomes attractive as rents increase, whereas Italy — which has a higher tax rate with more generous allowances — is a preferred location if rents earned are low.

It would take rather too much space to repeat with reference to investments earning a range of rents the decomposition of the previous section which dealt with marginal investments. Some element of competition probably ensures in any case that very large rents are not common, so the analysis here is repeated with rents being earned, but at a low level — just 10 per cent. Note that the results in this section are not directly comparable with those of the marginal investment. Whereas then the measure of dispersion was the standard deviation of required pre-tax rates of return in order to earn 5 per cent post-tax, here the measure is the standard deviation of average tax rates on 10 per cent of rent. Although the figures are not comparable, the interpretation remains the same — a fall in the standard deviation of tax rates faced by a company when making an investment decision indicates an improvement in capital export neutrality.

As with marginal investments, the degree of capital export neutrality is noticeably rather than dramatically improved by harmonising depreciation rates at all levels of inflation. However, in contrast to the marginal investment, harmonising tax rates (whilst keeping the base unharmonised) improves neutrality to a significant extent. Otherwise, the comments on Table 2.7 (the marginal investment case) can be repeated for Table 2.8. Simply abolishing withholding taxes has a large impact; moving to an exemption system further improves matters. A credit system proves to be preferable to the exemption system. By harmonising everything bar the base (column 7), the variance is again reduced by half compared to the current situation (column 1), but the difference between columns 6 and 7 is again very small, given that the latter harmonises tax rates, treatment of dividend payments and treatment of foreign source income, whereas the former simply standardises the last of these three aspects of the European tax system.

2.4 Conclusions

This chapter has extended a now standard model to calculate effective tax rates in two ways. First, it allowed for companies based in one country to invest in another. Secondly, it allowed companies to earn rent — profit over and above the minimum needed to satisfy shareholders.

This model was used to compare the dispersion of tax rates faced by a company located in one country investing either domestically or in another country. Taking one such company from each of the European Community Twelve, the average of the dispersion faced by each was interpreted as a measure of the degree of capital export non-neutrality, and the total dispersion in the matrix was identified as giving an indication of the degree of capital import non-neutrality. Four states of the world were considered — a marginal investment earning no rent, and a project earning a 10 per cent rent, both with no inflation and with 10 per cent inflation. Significant dispersions in effective tax rates were found; the consequence could easily be to distort commercial decisions, reducing Community-wide welfare.

A point of obvious interest is which country has the lowest effective tax rate. However there is no simple answer to the question — it depends on the assets and the finance for a particular investment, the country where the company making the investment is based, the inflation rate and the amount of profit made. For instance, taking a weighted average of assets, assuming a project to be financed by new

TABLE 2.8

Non-neutralities in the international tax system when a 10% rent is being earned: standard deviation of average tax rates on rent for companies resident in each country

	(1) Current Situation (mid 1989)		(2) Common Tax Base		(3) Common National Tax Rate (50%)		(4) Current Systems (credit/exemption)		(5) No Withholding Taxes — Exemption System		(6) Credit System		(7) Harmonise Everything Except the Base (1975 proposal)	
Inflation	0	10	0	10	0	10	0	10	0	10	0	10	0	10
BELGIUM	0.61	1.18	0.49	1.09	0.39	0.73	0.46	0.86	0.47	0.88	0.30	0.39	0.29	0.44
DENMARK	0.61	1.21	0.50	1.11	0.34	0.75	0.55	1.04	0.47	0.87	0.29	0.42	0.29	0.44
FRANCE	0.58	1.19	0.51	1.12	0.37	0.79	0.47	0.87	0.47	0.88	0.29	0.39	0.29	0.44
GERMANY	0.57	1.12	0.51	1.11	0.25	0.53	0.55	0.99	0.55	0.99	0.35	0.50	0.29	0.44
GREECE	0.65	1.19	0.50	1.10	0.42	0.73	0.50	0.92	0.47	0.87	0.30	0.39	0.29	0.44
IRELAND	0.60	1.24	0.55	1.18	0.33	0.75	0.49	0.91	0.49	0.91	0.49	0.91	0.29	0.44
ITALY	0.71	1.38	0.56	1.24	0.51	0.97	0.61	1.13	0.47	0.87	0.30	0.40	0.29	0.44
LUXEMBOURG	0.61	1.26	0.55	1.22	0.34	0.77	0.47	0.88	0.47	0.88	0.30	0.39	0.29	0.44
NETHERLANDS	0.60	1.23	0.53	1.15	0.36	0.79	0.48	0.89	0.48	0.89	0.31	0.48	0.29	0.44
PORTUGAL	0.56	1.15	0.49	1.09	0.33	0.73	0.48	0.89	0.48	0.89	0.28	0.40	0.29	0.44
SPAIN	0.60	1.23	0.55	1.20	0.33	0.69	0.48	0.89	0.48	0.89	0.30	0.47	0.29	0.44
UK	0.57	1.17	0.51	1.12	0.33	0.73	0.48	0.89	0.48	0.89	0.30	0.48	0.29	0.44
CEN	0.60	1.21	0.52	1.14	0.36	0.75	0.50	0.93	0.48	0.89	0.32	0.47	0.29	0.44
CIN	0.61	1.23	0.53	1.16	0.38	0.78	0.51	0.96	0.48	0.89	0.36	0.58	0.29	0.44

equity, and an inflation rate of zero per cent, it was found that if the profit on an investment was such that the providers of capital could be repaid, leaving some surplus (rent), a British company may wish to invest in Italy. Were the rent to be larger, the company should invest in the France; and if the rent were larger still, the optimal location might be Portugal — assuming that in the absence of tax, the same profit could be earned in each location.

In order to identify which aspects of the current international tax system cause the distortions, various reforms were tested on the model. Harmonising the tax base in each country reduced the distortion in all states, by a little. Harmonising the tax rates had little effect in the marginal investment case, but did have some effect for projects which earned a rent. Note that this does not mean that harmonising tax rates must *always* be of limited importance in any possible tax system, simply that this is so in the current system.

In contrast to these slightly negative results, it was found that the abolition of withholding taxes on the payment of dividends abroad — a measure with only relatively minor revenue consequences, in contrast to other reforms — had a significant impact at all levels of rent and inflation levels. This impact was further increased by harmonising the taxation of foreign source income either to an exemption or to a credit system (the latter produced the lower distortions). Indeed, the combination of simply abolishing withholding taxes and introducing a credit system in all countries had such a marked improvement on the distortions created by the tax system that it was hardly bettered by the reforms proposed by the Commission in 1975: harmonisation of tax rates, a common imputation system with completely harmonised rates and exemption from tax of foreign source income. In view of the political difficulties in implementing the Commission's proposals, the rather less sensitive route of adjusting only the taxation of international flows appears attractive.

NOTES

1. Capital export neutrality (CEN) and capital import neutrality (CIN) are defined in Chapter 1.
2. The precise rules for the operation of credit systems differ between countries. Alworth (1988) describes them in detail.
3. For the purposes of the model, information provided in European Regional Incentives (1988) is used.
4. Alworth (1988), who develops a similar model to the one summarised here but which only covers direct investment from the UK in Germany, allows for more vaired sources of finance.

CHAPTER 3

THE DISTORTION OF COMPANY DECISIONS BY THE TAX SYSTEM

The first chapter of this report laid out the principal ways in which the tax system could distort key business decisions. In particular, the choice about where to invest, and who invests, could be influenced by the tax system. The second chapter quantified the amount by which effective tax rates on rents can differ, and hence the incentive to locate production in less efficient countries, or for less efficient companies to gain an advantage in the European market by simple accident of birth.

However, by themselves the arguments given so far might not be thought strong enough to demonstrate the need to change the corporate tax system. The distortions caused by the tax system may only be theoretical; companies may not realise they exist, or the tax incentives to invest in particular countries may not be large enough to alter company behaviour. Alternatively companies may have developed accounting techniques and business structures which exploit loopholes in the existing tax structures.

Clearly, to assess the importance of non-neutralities in the tax system it is necessary to examine current business practice. Ideally, econometric techniques should be employed to analyse actual investment flows and relate them to existing tax incentives. However, there is insufficient data to allow this. An alternative is to examine the practices of those actually involved in investment decisions, and who therefore know from their own experience whether tax matters. To do this, the IFS commissioned the Confederation of British Industry to distribute a questionnaire to a sample of British companies. Respondents were asked a series of questions about whether tax considerations affected their business decisions. In addition, they were asked to comment on the desirability or otherwise of European intervention in the corporate tax system, and to evaluate possible reforms to the European corporate tax system. This chapter discusses the results. To anticipate our conclusions, tax considerations *do* appear to distort business decisions, and British companies *do* want harmonisation of European corporate tax systems.

3.1 The Sample

Few British companies are actually affected by the international tax system. No records are kept of UK investment overseas broken down by company size, but some indication of the concentration of overseas investment may be gleaned from the fact that over half of Britain's exports are accounted for by only 100 companies (*British Business,* 28 May 1982). Only 750 firms exported more than £5m worth of goods in 1980, and around 80 per cent of exports were by companies with related overseas companies. It seems reasonable to expect that investments are even more concentrated than exports, by just a few very large companies.

That being so, are the answers to the questionnaire a reasonable sample of those concerned with international tax? One hundred and seventy-three British companies completed the questionnaire. Of the 173 respondents, 48 had turnovers in excess of £500m. Only 209 companies in the UK satisfied that criterion at the end of 1987 and in early 1988 (Times, 1989). It therefore appears that around a quarter of the top 200 companies have responded to the questionnaire — certainly adequate to give some indication of the attitudes of that group, and hence the attitudes of those UK companies most likely to have interests in tax systems other than that of the UK. Some characteristics of the companies responding to the questionnaire are given in Table 3.1.

TABLE 3.1

Composition of the sample of UK companies

Turnover	Business of Company				UK Turnover	UK Investment
(£'s)	Industry	Retail	Services	Other	(% of global turnover)	(% of global investment)
0–1m	5	1	3	1	71.8	78.6
1–5m	15	1	2	2	77.1	95.4
5–20m	10	2	4	2	72.4	86.9
20–50m	16	1	3	3	58.0	75.9
50–100m	8	1	5	1	67.1	87.7
100–200m	11	1	6	–	69.6	83.8
200–500m	10	–	4	2	62.1	66.9
500 +	26	7	9	5	56.6	65.9
Total	101	14	36	16	64.7	77.8

As well as the representativeness of the sample, another issue is whether the answers are adequate reflections of the actual actions and responses of the companies to the international tax system. As in all such questionnaires, there clearly is a need for some caution. The experience of one person may not reflect the complexities of a decision made by the company as a whole. Their opinions about the importance of tax may differ from other members of the company. In addition, the mere fact of being asked specifically about taxes may raise the profile of tax as an influence on investment in the mind of the respondent. Answers may tend to exaggerate the importance of issues which are in fact mildly irritating; exaggerating the scale of a problem is more likely to get public policy changed — although it is not necessarily the case that companies do want change.

However, there is reason to believe that the responses to this survey were reliable. Respondents were asked to indicate their job-titles. Around 45 per cent of respondents were directors, presumably in a good position to indicate the true importance of tax.[1] Only 12 per cent were tax-managers.[2]

The questionnaire was in any case designed as far as possible so as to make misleading statements unlikely. For instance, instead of merely asking respondents whether they knew of other countries with lower taxes and thus competitive advantages, they were also asked to name the countries. In some cases, the same question was asked twice, at different points in the questionnaire, and worded somewhat differently.

In general, it seems reasonable to assume that when a respondent says that tax is a major influence on a particular investment issues, he or she is likely to mean it. Therefore, as the sample of respondents is a significant proportion of those influenced by tax systems other than that of the UK, it seems that the answers to the questionnaire are of value.

The questions asked in the questionnaire fall into three groups. One is the central issue of whether tax influences the location of investment, or who undertakes an investment. The second is the structure of investments; how they are financed, the impact of thin capitalisation and transfer pricing rules and the use of intermediaries. Such issues can affect efficiency in two ways; they tie up real resources in coping with or avoiding complex regulations, and they may also result in inefficient business and financial structures in international companies. The third series of questions asked were about the opinions of the respondents as regards harmonisation.

3.2 Capital Import and Export Non-Neutrality

Companies were asked whether taxes and grants influenced them when deciding in which country to locate an investment. Respondents were allowed to say whether tax was *always, usually, sometimes* or *never* a relevant consideration and a major factor.

The location of a production plant is quite likely to be distorted by tax. Fifty-five per cent of those who answered the question said taxes and grants were *always* a relevant consideration, and 76 per cent said that they were at least *usually* relevant. Around 53 per cent of those who answered said that they were at least *usually* a major factor.

However, around 40 per cent of respondents did not answer the question. This may reflect the fact that many respondents were too small to have overseas investments, or had not invested abroad for some other reason. More relevant estimates of the importance of tax are achieved by limiting the sample to some extent. Therefore two sets of figures will be sometimes be presented. One is the full sample. The other includes only those companies with a turnover of over £50 million; and of these, those with more than 90 per cent of their sales or 90 per cent of their investment over the last five years in the UK are excluded.[3] As a result of these restrictions, the second group is limited to those companies aware of the transnational tax system, and also who may find their corporate plans influenced by the tax system. This subgroup is given more attention, and is labelled the *restricted* sample, as opposed to the *full* one.

As Table 3.2 shows, of this *restricted* sample, 48 per cent of those who answered think that tax and grant are *always* a relevant consideration; 76 per cent think they are at least *usually* a relevant consideration. None think that they are *never* relevant, and 43 per cent think they are at least *usually* a major factor.

TABLE 3.2

In deciding in which country to locate a new production plant, how often are tax and grants a relevant consideration or a major factor in your location decision (% of restricted sample who answered)

	Always	Usually	Sometimes	Never	No answer
relevant consideration	47.8	28.3	23.9	0	25.8
major factor	18.9	24.3	40.5	16.2	40.3

These answers would seem to indicate that the international corporate tax system *does* influence the location of direct foreign investment. The lack of capital export neutrality in the international tax system therefore probably does lead to inefficient resource allocation. However, a related question concerning how investment plans would change if corporate taxes were harmonised was also asked later in the questionnaire. Respondents were asked to indicate their position on a scale 1 (not at all) to 5 (substantially). Answers are given in Table 3.3.

TABLE 3.3

How do you think your current investment plans would change if the total future corporate tax charge you will face on the returns was totally unaffected by the location of the investments? (% of restricted sample who answered)

Not at all--substantially					no answer
1	2	3	4	5	
29.3	37.9	20.7	10.3	1.7	6.5

The second question appears to indicate that the distortion caused by the international tax system is much less. Part of the explanation of this apparent contradiction lies in the non-response rate. The last column of each table shows the percentage of the sample under consideration who did not respond to a question. While many did not answer the first question about whether tax influenced investment decisions, few failed to answer the question about whether their investment plans would change. The reason is obvious — not all companies have invested abroad and so they did not answer the question on their influences. Consequently, harmonising tax would have no affect on their current investment plans. Of those who did *not* answer the question on whether taxes and grants for new production plants were ever relevant, over 80 per cent answered either 1 or 2 when asked to indicate how their investment plans would *change* if tax had no influence.

The appropriate way of interpreting these results therefore seems to be that where companies have, for whatever reason, invested abroad, tax *has* been an important influence. However, not all firms have undertaken much foreign investment. Therefore changes to *current* investment plans will be limited.

So far, the questions have been focused on capital export neutrality (CEN); that is, whether a particular company faces the same tax regime irrespective of the location of its production. It is more difficult to get evidence from companies about the impact on them following from the absence of capital import neutrality (CIN) — all firms competing in the same market facing the same overall tax regime. This is primarily because the country in which the sale takes place need not be the country in which production takes place. Sixty per cent of the restricted sample exported goods (normally in addition to selling through a local subsidiary), which implies that CIN is unlikely to hold unless all countries have the same tax system. The following question was asked:

> In deciding in which country to locate [investments] are there any countries in which you would not normally invest because your competitors in that country would face a lower total corporate tax charge than your own company?

Of the *restricted* sample of large firms with overseas interests, only one claimed to have been so influenced by tax in this that they did not invest in a production plant, and one (different) firm noted the same problem with a sales outlet. However, a lower awareness of capital import non-neutrality than of distortions in the decision about where to invest is likely, even if they are equally important. Firms which invest overseas explicitly face the choice about where to invest, and so calculate the tax situations. In contrast, the only explicit evidence that might indicate capital import non-neutrality is that some firms can produce goods cheaper than others, or find some project more profitable than others. Such situations can be caused by factors other than tax.

Finally, companies were asked about which aspects of the international tax system influenced their business decisions. Results are given in Table 3.4.

A simple ranking of concern would seem to be that tax rates were most important, followed by withholding tax rates and depreciation rates, and then by tax loss provisions. Grants have the least effect, although even these are at least *usually* a major factor for a third of the respondents. An ordinal ranking should not be allowed to obscure the fact that companies consider all these aspects of the tax system to be influential in their location decisions.

It is interesting to compare these responses with the results given in Tables 2.7 and 2.8. There it was argued that tax rates had a rather limited effect on the dispersion of effective tax rates so that harmonisation of rates would not greatly reduce the absence of CEN. By contrast, companies think that tax rates are of considerable importance in distorting business decisions. The same is true of depreciation provisions, although both tables assign an important role to withholding taxes.

TABLE 3.4

How often are the following a relevant consideration or a major factor when deciding the location of an investment? (% of respondents of restricted sample who answered each section; non-response rate in final column)

		Always	Usually	Sometimes	Never	No answer
Tax Rates	relevant consideration	56.5	22.6	17.7	3.2	0
	major factor	30.8	21.2	34.6	13.5	16.1
Withholding Tax Rates	relevant consideration	39.7	37.9	17.2	5.2	6.4
	major factor	18.5	25.9	40.7	14.8	12.9
Depreciation Provisions	relevant consideration	36.1	27.9	26.2	9.8	1.6
	major factor	22.6	11.3	37.7	28.3	14.5
Tax Loss Provisions	relevant consideration	34.5	29.3	29.3	6.9	6.4
	major factor	14.5	20.0	41.8	23.6	11.3
Automatic Grants	relevant consideration	25.4	25.4	40.7	8.5	4.8
	major factor	12.7	21.8	47.3	18.2	11.3
Discretionary Grants	relevant consideration	25.9	22.4	43.1	‚8.6	6.4
	major factor	12.5	21.4	44.6	21.4	9.7

3.3 The Structure of International Operations

The decision about where to locate an investment is one of the more visible aspects of tax distortion. It is not the only consequence of a distortionary tax system. The structure and finance of the project may be determined by tax.

Branch and Subsidiary

Conventional wisdom has it that when starting a new project in a foreign country, a company should use a branch. This enables the start-up losses of the project to be written off against the parent's profits. Once profits are being made, the branch should be transformed into a subsidiary by incorporation, allowing the parent to retain profits in the subsidiary so as to be able to repatriate profit as and when the parent desires. Of the sample of restricted companies, the choice of branch and subsidiary was as in Table 3.5. Most operate through subsidiaries.

However, tax was not the only reason for choosing subsidiaries. When asked by how much the choice was determined by tax, on a

TABLE 3.5

How far are your existing operations organised through subsidiaries rather than branches? (% of restricted sample who answered)

Proportion of operations organised through subsidiaries					no answer
less than 20%	21% to 40%	41% to 60%	61% to 80%	more than 80%	
9.7	6.5	6.5	4.8	72.6	0

scale of 1 (not at all) to 5 (substantially), the average was 2.7. Over 30 per cent of the sample answered 4 or 5, but 50 per cent answered 1 or 2. There are, therefore, reasons for structuring foreign operations through subsidiaries to do with non-tax related issues. Nevertheless, tax plays *some* role in most cases.

Intermediaries

By repatriating profits from abroad to the parent company via an intermediary company in a third country, it is sometimes possible to reduce total taxes paid. This is because of the UK's use of a *credit* system. The UK charges tax on profits earned abroad only when the tax already paid on the profits to the source country is less than would have been paid had the project been located in Britain. However, no refund is given when overseas tax is greater than would have been paid were the investment in the UK. If a UK parent company has two projects, one in a high tax country (X), and one in a low tax country (Y), it will pay no tax to the UK on the investment in X, but will pay on those profits earned in Y. Were the company to divert profits from the two subsidiaries to a company based in a country which *exempts* foreign source income (i.e. charges no tax), and send the *combined* profits from the two subsidiaries to the parent, it is only charged tax on the average amount by which foreign tax is less than UK tax. Table 3.6 shows the extent to which this kind of situation occurs.

TABLE 3.6

How far are your existing overseas operations organised routed via intermediaries in another country? (% of restricted sample who answered)

Proportion of operations routed via intermediaries					no answer
less than 20%	21% to 40%	41% to 60%	61% to 80%	more than 80%	
78.3	10.0	5.0	5.0	1.7	3.2

The extent to which this phenomenon takes place is perhaps rather less than might be expected. There are two explanations. One is that 'averaging' is less beneficial than in the past due to the reduction in the UK tax rate. The second is that this table may be misleading, in that 'less than 20 per cent' does not mean zero. The sample was asked to name the countries in which it used intermediaries to route profits to the UK, and 52 per cent of the sample gave an answer — presumably many firms use intermediaries a little, but few route a *high* proportion of their profits through intermediaries.

The most popular country in which to locate intermediaries is the Netherlands. Of those with intermediaries, 28 per cent had them in the Netherlands (possibly more — 25 per cent of those with intermediaries said that there were too many to list). The Netherlands has an exemption system, so using an intermediary based there may reduce UK taxes. The Dutch government benefits from being used in this way, because it levies a withholding tax on profits transferred to the UK; though not at a high enough level to remove the attractiveness of performing this financial manoeuvre (the withholding tax is 5 per cent if the UK parent owns 25 per cent or more of the Dutch company).

When asked how much this choice of using an intermediary was affected by tax, of those using them the average response was surprisingly low — 2.8 on a scale of 1 (not at all) to 5 (substantially). Of the restricted sample of large companies with overseas interests, including those with no intermediaries the average response was 2.3.

Finance of Investments

Providing finance for a new investment can be complicated by tax systems in many ways. In addition to the normal distortions between debt, retentions and new equity finance if the funds are both raised and used domestically, other issues arise for international operations. The questionnaire asked several questions to determine the degree to which foreign subsidiaries were financed by the parent and the degree to which debt finance was used.

For international operations, it is clear that where tax rates are high, the distortion in favour of debt — given the tax deductibility of interest payments — is also high. Thus it should be expected that in these cases, projects will tend to be financed by borrowing. If the parent's tax rate is lower than the tax rate in the country in which an investment is located, then the parent will be inclined to lend to its overseas operation, and so extract profits from overseas in tax deductible form and generate taxable profits in the low tax residence country. In addition, dividend payments tend to attract higher withholding taxes than interest payments. Thus, for finance provided by the parent, the international tax system encourages debt finance over equity. To limit the extent to which this occurs, 'thin-capitalisation' rules exist, which force at least some finance to be provided by equity.

A further problem, specifically relating to the UK-style imputation system, is to make sure that sufficient profits are declared by the parent, in order to claim all possible ACT relief. As noted in the discussion on mergers in Chapter 1, if too high a proportion of profits is derived from foreign subsidiaries, parent companies end up paying more ACT than can be offset against their domestic mainstream tax liability. By *lending* money to overseas operations, (thin-capitalisation rules permitting) profits are generated domestically, and this problem reduced (provided, of course, that the rate of withholding on interest is sufficiently low).

Table 3.7 illustrates the amount of local borrowing used (on average) when making an investment in a *new* country. There appears to be a tendency to try to *avoid* local borrowing in new countries. The reason is clear: during a start-up period in a new country there are unlikely

TABLE 3.7

When you make an investment in a new country, what proportion, on average, of the investment is financed by 'local' borrowing, rather than by capital injected directly or indirectly by the holding company? (% of restricted sample who answered)

	Proportion of investment financed by local borrowing					
less than 20%	21% to 40%	41% to 60%	61% to 80%	more than 80%		no answer
29.3	15.5	29.3	13.8	12.1		6.5

TABLE 3.8

On average, what proportion of your new investment in foreign countries already operated in is financed locally rather than by new capital injected directly or indirectly by the holding company? (% of restricted sample who answered)

	Proportion of overseas investment financed locally					
less than 20%	21% to 40%	41% to 60%	61% to 80%	more than 80%		no answer
19.7	11.5	14.8	14.8	39.3		1.6

TABLE 3.9

Of the proportion which is financed locally, on average, how much is local borrowing rather than retained earnings? (% of restricted sample who answered)

	Proportion of local finance which is borrowing					no answer
less than 20%	21% to 40%	41% to 60%	61% to 80%	more than 80%		
21.7	20.0	28.3	16.7	13.3		3.2

to be sufficient taxable profits being generated in that country against which interest payments can be set. In contrast, when a new investment is in a country where there is already a presence by the company, there is a greater use of local finance (Table 3.8), and this tends to be borrowing rather than retained earnings (Table 3.9). One of the reasons may be the influence of ACT. To borrow in the UK in order to inject capital into the subsidiary *reduces* UK taxable profit earned in the UK, and so may result in insufficient profits against which to offset ACT payments.

Companies were asked to indicate the role of tax in all these situations, on a scale of 1 (not at all) to 5 (substantially). On the decision as to whether to finance a new investment in a new country by raising the finance locally, the average role of tax was 3. When investing in a country in which there already was an existing investment, the role of tax in determining the financial structure was 3.1. On the decision as to use of borrowing or retaining earnings to finance the new investment in a country where there already was a presence, tax exerted an influence of 2.6. All of these results suggest an important influence of tax on financial structure.

Companies were also asked to give some indication of how the holding company (parent) raised money to finance an investment by a subsidiary abroad. Table 3.10 shows that both borrowing and

TABLE 3.10

Of the proportion which is financed by the holding company, on average how much is in the form of borrowing from the holding company rather than in the form of equity? (% of restricted sample who answered)

	Proportion of holding company finance which is borrowing					no answer
less than 20%	21% to 40%	41% to 60%	61% to 80%	more than 80%		
25.0	21.7	15.0	18.3	20.0		3.2

equity are used, with a bimodal distribution being apparent — companies tend to use one method of finance or the other. Tax again plays a significant role (an influence of 3.1 on a scale of 1 to 5).

Finally, respondents were given the opportunity to answer a question as to *how* tax influenced their choices. Some were quite illuminating. A selection is given below.

'By the use of loans it is effectively possible to choose between paying overseas tax or UK tax'

'General policy is to maximise debt in high tax jurisdictions'

'If tax rates [are] higher than [in the] UK it pays to borrow locally rather than to remit dividends on equity'

'It is essential that overseas subsidiaries are financed by local borrowing, provided that the interest is tax deductible, in order to maximise over time UK profits against which to offset ACT relief'.

These comments perhaps illustrate more effectively than any tabulations could the pivotal role that tax pays in the structuring and financing of international operations.

3.4 What Companies Think About Corporate Tax Harmonisation

A series of questions was asked to assess the opinions of respondents with regard to the desirable characteristics a European tax system *should* have. Should all companies face the same tax rate? Which is the more important, capital import or capital export neutrality? Should we want neutrality at all costs, or should underdeveloped regions be favoured? Perhaps even more controversial is the 'fortress Europe' issue: do British companies want the tax system to discriminate against the non-European world? Respondents were also asked about their opinions concerning harmonisation — should it be of base, system, rates, credit or exemption etc?

An objection could be made that many of these questions are being asked of respondents who are not really qualified to answer. Businesses opinions about the favouring of Europe over the rest of the world are presumably coloured by the fact that such a policy would lessen competition in Europe, and so boost profits — at the expense of consumers. Even were this view true (and in fact the answers show that such cynicism is misplaced) European business opinions are an important influence on the development of the 1992 programme.

Respondents were asked whether, *within* the EC, there should be tax incentives for an EC company to invest in one member country rather than another. This identifies whether they believe that capital export neutrality (CEN) should be an aim of the corporate tax harmonisation process. Of those large capital exporting companies who answered the question, an overwhelming 84 per cent supported CEN. In the full sample of 173 firms, the support for capital export neutrality was scarcely less emphatic — 81 per cent in favour.

However, when asked whether there should be incentives for a company resident in the EC to invest within the EC rather than outside it, a lower proportion, 54 per cent of the subsample and 56 per cent of the full sample, were in favour. This might be regarded as inconsistent with the previous response. It is true that the benefits of global CEN are global, and would therefore be shared globally, but the benefits of purely European CEN would be divided throughout Europe. Apparently sharing the benefits with other Europeans is more acceptable to a minority of repondents than sharing larger benefits world-wide.

An eleven to one majority in favour of all similar EC companies (including domestic companies) *operating* in a given EC country facing the same *total* corporate tax charge on their operations in that country (in other words, the narrow interpretation of CIN) was recorded in the restricted sample. In the full sample, the total was nine to one. Extending the question to cover *non*-EC companies reduced the majority if favour of this form of import neutrality to 78 per cent of the smaller sample, and 77 per cent of the full sample. Again a small bias against non-Europeans is evident in the answers of some respondents.

Given the overwhelming support for equal treatment of those investing in and those investing from each member state of the Community it is hardly surprising that the general principle — that all companies *selling* in a given EC country should face the same total corporate tax charge on operations to produce and market that product (which is the more general definition of capital import neutrality), is favoured. Over 82 per cent of the full sample, and 80 per cent of the subsample were in favour. Again, extending the question to consider non-EC companies reduced the percentages in favour, to 64 per cent in each sample.

TABLE 3.11

How would you evaluate the following possible reforms to the corporation tax systems of EC countries? (% of those answering each section; non-response rate in final column)

	Sample	Necessary	Desirable	Unimportant	Undesirable	No answer
The creation of a	Full	26.3	62.3	6.6	4.8	3.5
uniform taxable base	Restricted	21.0	67.7	6.5	4.8	0
A band for	Full	19.8	72.5	4.8	3.0	3.5
Corporation tax rates	Restricted	11.5	83.6	3.3	1.6	1.6
An imputation	Full	18.9	66.5	11.0	3.7	5.2
system with EC franked income	Restricted	14.5	80.6	4.8	0	0
Standardisation of	Full	22.2	68.9	7.2	1.8	3.5
withholding tax rates	Restricted	22.6	71.0	6.5	0	0
Exemption of all	Full	17.1	66.5	14.0	2.4	5.2
foreign source income from the EC	Restricted	9.7	75.8	12.9	1.6	0
Credit system with	Full	13.8	47.2	30.2	8.8	8.1
averaging for EC income	Restricted	17.7	59.7	21.0	1.6	0

The Type of Harmonisation

Respondents were asked their opinions on the appropriate direction for harmonisation. Answers are given in Table 3.11 for both the full sample, and the restricted sample of large firms with overseas interests.

Obviously, harmonisation of base and of rates is favoured by our respondents by a massive majority. Between 88 and 96 per cent are in favour of harmonisation (in that they answer it is either necessary or desirable) depending on which sample and which aspect of harmonisation is being considered, as against between 2 and 5 per cent thinking the principle of harmonisation is undesirable. Agreement that a common imputation system, with credits given regardless of the residence of the shareholder, is scarcely less favoured. Not one of the sample of large companies opposed such a move; 95 per cent of them would applaud it. This is precisely the *system* that the Commission proposed in 1975 (although popularity for that proposal would presumably be lessened if the rather high tax rate of 45 to 55 per cent were specified in the question).

Regarding the treatment of foreign source income, it is obvious that the standardisation of withholding taxes within the EC on interest and dividends is strongly supported by British business. The choice between exemption and credit with averaging systems is not so clear-cut; both are favoured, so presumably either would be approved of, but respondents were not asked to actually state a preference between the two.

3.5 Conclusions

The following conclusions can be drawn from our survey of UK companies.

1. Of those companies which have invested abroad, tax has been a significant factor in deciding where to invest.

2. The *structure* of overseas investment is substantially influenced by tax — in particular, the use of intermediaries and the choice of using subsidiaries rather than branches.

3. Tax issues are also important in determining both the source of finance (from the parent or raised locally) and the type of finance (borrowing or equity). The importance of tax in this area is perhaps greater than in any other aspect of transnational business.

4. British companies are strongly in favour of harmonisation, although the majority in favour of harmonising effective tax rates between Europeans and non-Europeans was lower.

5. Harmonisation of the base, rates, system, withholding taxes and treatment of foreign source income is considered desirable by British companies. There is no strong preference as to the choice between exemption of foreign source income and a credit system.

The evidence of distortions caused by the European tax system is clear; the evidence of British business believing the harmonisation of European corporate taxation to be desirable is overwhelming. The last two chapters have demonstrated, first, that the current tax treatment of transnational projects is not neutral and, secondly, that these non-neutralities do distort business behaviour. Consequently there is a case for corporate tax harmonisation within the European Community. The next chapter considers possible forms that harmonisation might take, and discusses the possibility of agreement ever being reached among the twelve member states.

NOTES

1. These figures are somewhat biased by the inclusion of the very small companies, whose opinions may not be of much importance. However, of those large firms with turnovers in excess of £100m, the proportion of directors was almost as high. Nineteen respondents were tax managers, whereas twenty-nine were directors (including five managing directors), thirteen were financial managers, and five were from the planning departments. Six gave other responses, and ten gave no answer.

2. Most of these were the *group* tax managers, who presumably do in any case have a significant influence on business decisions.

3. This may bias the sample. Some large companies may choose to invest in the UK, despite being large enough to invest in other countries, because the tax treatment of profits in the UK is more favourable than elsewhere. However, it seems to us more likely the absence of international investment by a large company reflects the absence of any motive to do so, rather than preferential UK tax treatment. The lack of a motive probably indicates that there has been no need to spend time learning about tax treatment of international investment, so answers are misleading.

CHAPTER 4

TOWARDS HARMONISATION

The various threads of the report are drawn together in this chapter, in which a number of different options for the reform of European corporate taxes are analysed in some detail. The underlying theme of this chapter is the distinction between the economic aims and political feasibility of harmonisation. Chapter 1 discussed in some detail how corporate taxes may introduce inefficiencies (and hence welfare losses) in the global allocation of goods and services. However, it was also argued that the only way to completely eliminate such inefficiencies was to have a single European tax system, to be faced by all companies based within the European Community. Any report which advocated such a tax, however, would be begging for obscurity given the apparent lack of political will for such an arrangement which would also completely remove the sovereignty of national governments to design their own corporate tax systems. In this chapter we begin by describing such a system before going on to analyse the possible trade-offs between economic efficiency and national sovereignty under less sweeping reforms. Two other groups of issues which must also be simultaneously considered are first, the administrative and compliance costs of alternative regimes and second, the extent to which they would mitigate the problems of present regimes, such as transfer pricing, thin capitalisation, start-up losses and transnational mergers.

Before discussing possible harmonised corporate tax systems, we summarise the aims and requirements of the eventual regime. We then discuss a number of possible different routes towards some degree of harmonisation in the context of these aims and requirements. The routes chosen reflect to some extent the arguments and results already presented in the report, notably in Chapter 2. That is, concentration is focused mainly on reforms to the taxation of cross-border flows, rather than any specific reforms to tax bases or rates. There are two reasons for this emphasis. The first is that the taxation of such flows plays a very important part in forming the economic inefficiencies discussed at length in this report. Tables 2.7 and 2.8 provide evidence of the distorting effects of withholding taxes on dividends paid abroad, and the importance of whether countries operate an exemption or credit system on foreign source income. The second is that the taxation of such flows is relatively unimportant in revenue terms for governments. In particular, countries such as the UK raise virtually no revenue from operating a credit, rather than an exemption, system. The taxation of such flows is irrelevant for the vast majority of corporate activity which operates only domestically. If the taxation of only these transnational flows were dictated by the Commission (or, rather, unanimously agreed by the Council of Ministers), national governments would maintain much of the right to set their own tax systems.

4.1 Summarising the Aims and Requirements of Harmonisation

The aims and requirements of harmonisation are discussed under four headings:

(i) Economic Efficiency

There are two kinds of economic inefficiency which arise because different countries operate different corporate tax systems. Probably the most important is the absence of capital export neutrality (CEN). CEN would hold for companies resident in a given country if the tax burden faced by those companies were the same irrespective of in which country the activities of those companies were located. Thus, for example, a UK company would face the same effective tax rate on a particular investment regardless of whether it set up the plant in the UK, France or Italy. Suppose that, for some reason, this company can produce more cheaply in Italy. Then, in the presence of CEN, it will clearly set up the plant in Italy. In the absence of CEN, however, it might be the case that the company would face such a high tax rate by producing in Italy that it would find it more profitable after tax to undertake the project in the UK. Given that this raises the costs of production there is a clear economic inefficiency and welfare loss which arises in the absence of CEN. Note, however, that the inefficiency arises only if profitability depends on the location of production.

The second type of inefficiency is rather more subtle, and, there is reason to suspect, probably less common. In Chapter 1 it was referred to as the absence of capital import neutrality (CIN). CIN holds if all competitors in the same market face the same underlying tax burden.[1] Thus, for example, suppose that only Renault and Fiat compete to sell cars in Europe. Suppose also that Renault is a more efficient producer and, in the presence of CIN, can therefore sell cars more cheaply, thus capturing a larger share of the market. If CIN does not hold, however, it may be the case that Renault faces such a high tax burden that it is forced to increase the price at which it sells cars to above that charged by Fiat, thus conceding most of the market to Fiat. In this case there is again a clear welfare loss. The reason why the absence of CIN may be less important than the absence of CEN is that a welfare loss following from the absence of CIN can only arise if Renault just happens to be more efficient than Fiat, irrespective of where production actually takes place.[2] Whilst this is possible, it seems unlikely that the difference in efficiency between European firms is as large as the differences in the productivity of work forces and in transport costs. These two inefficiencies provide the major economic reasons for moving towards a more harmonised system of corporate taxes in Europe.

(ii) Political Acceptability

The main disadvantage of harmonisation is the degree to which national governments need to give up the right to set taxes on residents of their country or on activities which take place in their country. Several aspects of this issue should be noted. First, the issue of sovereignty can be applied to three categories: the right to tax activities taking place in a country (the sovereignty of the source country); the right to tax residents of a country who produce and make profits in a different country (the sovereignty of the resident country); and, third, the right to tax residents who operate only domestically (domestic sovereignty). Giving up the first and second of these rights is considerably less important in practice than giving up the third. This is one reason why it was earlier argued that reforms which only affected transnational flows would be much easier to accept than reforms to the tax base which affected all activities in each country.

It is also necessary to distinguish two forms of political acceptability. The first is that governments require at least a share of the tax revenue arising from particular activities. However, this may occur even if a national government gives up the right to determine what tax regime applies to the activities or residents in its country. For example, if all corporate taxes were levied on a source basis, the residence country may still be offered a share of the revenue collected. In fact, moving the system either to a source or to a residence base is unlikely to be politically acceptable without introducing some compensation to the country no longer taxing the income. Some member states would be willing to introduce such a reform, but with unanimity still required in the Council of Ministers for tax matters, it is hard to see any convincing reason for potential losers to not exercise their veto.

The second aspect of sovereignty is the right of a government to set the tax regime applying to activities in, or residents of, its country. A government may wish to exercise this right, for example, to encourage inward investment. However, encouraging inward investment is an example of precisely what is precluded by the economic aims of harmonisation since it is completely opposed to CEN. In many of the reforms considered below, either residence or source countries would be required to give up this form of sovereignty: for example, if taxation is on a source base, the residence country cannot add to the tax burden imposed by the source country, although it might share in some of the revenue collected.

To summarise: two types of distinction are necessary. The first is that wholly domestic operations (which, by definition, only one government may tax) should be distinguished from transnational operations. The second is that the 'right' of a government to share in the tax revenue collected on certain profits does not necessarily imply that each government must be free to determine the overall effective tax regime applying to activities in, or residents of, its country.

(iii) Administration and Compliance Costs

Very different administrative and compliance costs could arise in various possible reforms. Under current systems, these costs are kept at a reasonably low level (although anti-avoidance provisions introduce complexity and hence additional costs). Thus, for example, the source country (where production takes place) would normally impose its own tax system on all activities in that country. If the activity takes place through a subsidiary of a foreign parent company the parent company may either be exempt or will face a further charge based on repatriated dividends. In this case, there is therefore only one tax base to be calculated by the company concerned. Under a unitary tax system however, there are potentially a large number of different tax bases to be calculated. If each country charges tax on a proportion of Europe-wide taxable profits (say), defined according to its own tax system, then not only does that country need details of all the company's operations in Europe (which it currently does not need), but the company or group concerned will need to calculate its Europe-wide profits under as many different tax systems as the number of countries in which it operates. Given such a multiplication of administrative and compliance costs such a system could only work if the tax bases of the different countries were very similar.

(iv) Other Issues

Four other issues arise which include elements of economic efficiency, political acceptability and administrative and compliance costs. The first two are transfer pricing and thin capitalisation.[3] Both of these may be used by companies to reduce the total size of their tax burden, although in the process they may increase administrative and compliance costs, cause a reallocation of revenues from one national government to another and also lead to further economic inefficiencies by, for example, encouraging too heavy reliance on debt finance from the parent, rather than raising revenue locally (which may be cheaper in the absence of tax). A system which did not allow the tax burden to be reduced in these ways (by taxing Europe-wide profits) would therefore overcome all of these problems.

Two final issues are the treatment of losses arising in a project starting up in a new country, and the degree to which the tax system discourages mergers between companies resident in different countries. Clearly economic distortions are created if start-up losses can be claimed against existing tax bills if they arise in one country but not if they arise in another. This is, in fact, a particularly common cause of capital export non-neutrality. Distortions may also arise if possible benefits from economies of scale cannot be used because mergers are discouraged.

4.2 General Approaches to Harmonisation

Before discussing detailed reforms, it is helpful to identify the main options for any set of tax regimes and to outline the strategy used below. In particular two important distinctions are apparent in the options discussed. They are the distinction between taxes at source and at residence and, secondly, the distinction between a country (normally the residence country) taxing Europe-wide profits or just the profits which are repatriated in the form of dividends or interest.

The distinction between source and residence based taxation essentially mirrors the aims of CIN and CEN. As discussed in Chapter 1, CIN is achieved if taxation is only in the source country (i.e. where production takes place) since two companies resident in different countries can compete on equal terms in the country with the lowest effective tax rate. By contrast, CEN is achieved by taxing according to the tax regime of the residence country; clearly, if a company faced the effective tax rate of its country of residence wherever it invested, CEN would be achieved. One of the principal difficulties in designing efficient harmonised tax systems is this dichotomy between aiming for CIN (and hence source-based taxation) or CEN (and hence residence-based taxation). As noted elsewhere, we suspect that the absence of CEN may be currently leading to greater inefficiencies, and so we discuss some reforms which are aimed at a residence base. However, administratively, a source-based tax is easier to implement and we discuss this option as well. An important distinction which should be noted here is that achieving CEN by a residence based tax means that any company faces the same effective tax rate wherever it invests; it does *not* mean, however, that all countries need to have the same statutory tax rate — it is simply that the only relevant tax regime is that of the residence country. A similar comment applies to achieving CIN through source-based tax.

A second important distinction is the tax base used by each country. If the tax base includes all profits made by the group in Europe, then generally several administrative complications of international tax disappear (at least for activities in Europe), notably transfer pricing and thin capitalisation. This is simply because all activities are lumped together — there is no advantage to declaring a taxable profit in one country rather than another. This would be the case, for example, with a unitary tax system as currently exists in the US (see for example, McClure, 1989). However, if tax is levied only on profits arising within a country or on profits repatriated to that country in the form of dividends or interest, problems such as transfer pricing and thin capitalisation assume considerable practical importance. In addition, potentially important distortions to company decisions might be induced by the additional tax liability generated by repatriating dividends or interest if there is a credit system in the residence country. For example, Hines and Hubbard (1989) suggest that most US multinationals avoid repatriating profits in order to avoid additional US tax.

In the specific reforms discussed below, we therefore begin with four possible regimes in which Europe-wide profits are taxed although only the first three avoid transfer pricing and thin capitalisation problems. We also consider unitary tax, which also taxes all European profits together. These modifications require greater change from the current situation than the other reforms which we consider, and which, possibly as a result, may be seen to be more likely to be politically acceptable. It should also be noted that taxing only repatriations can generally be done at a lower administrative cost.

4.3 Specific reforms

It is now possible to discuss how various possible reforms measure up to the aims and requirements that have been set out. Before beginning, it may be well to set one's mind in a frame of healthy pessimism since no system scores full marks on all of the criteria set out above. Having said that, however, and bearing in mind that some trade-offs between the various criteria are more a matter of political judgement than economic analysis, some reforms do meet the objectives of harmonisation better than others.

A summary of the reforms considered and how well they meet the criteria is given in Tables 4.1 and 4.2. The first two columns of Table 4.1 investigate the degree to which CEN and CIN are achieved. As pointed out above (and in more detail in Chapter 1) these only arise if

TABLE 4.1

Economic Efficiency versus Sovereignty

	Tax system	Economic Efficiency		Sovereignty		
		Rent depends on location of		Degree of sovereignty in		
		production	parent company residence	country of production	country of residence	domestic
i	Single European CT	FULL	FULL	0	0	0
ii	CT in shareholder residence location	FULL	FULL	0	0	10
iii	CT in parent company location	FULL	NO CIN	0	10	10
iv	CT *mainly* in parent company resience location	NOT FULLY CEN	NO CIN	4	7	10
v	CT in the parent company residence location for repatriations	NOT FULLY CEN	NO CIN	5	6	10
vi	Unitary tax	NO CEN	MOSTLY CIN	7	2	9
vii	CT in location of production	NO CEN	FULL	8	0	10

TABLE 4.2

Administrative and Compliance Costs and Other Factors

Tax system	Administration				Other Problems		
	Costs to authorities in country of:						
	production	parent company residence	s/holder residence	costs to company	Transfer pricing/thin capitalisation	Start-up losses	Mergers
i Single European CT	–	VERY GOOD	–	VERY GOOD	–	–	–
ii CT in s/holder residence location	GOOD	FAIR	FAIR	POOR	–	–	–
iii CT in parent co. residence location	GOOD	FAIR	GOOD	FAIR	–	–	–
iv CT *mainly* in parent co. residence location	GOOD	BAD	GOOD	BAD	YES	YES	MAYBE
v CT in parent co. residence location for repatriations	GOOD	FAIR	GOOD	GOOD	YES	YES	YES
vi Unitary tax	FAIR	FAIR	GOOD	VERY BAD	–	–	–
vii CT in location of production	GOOD	NONE	GOOD	GOOD	YES	YES	YES

economic profitability or rent varies according to the location of production or residence, respectively. When the rent depends on the location of production, inefficiencies are likely to occur because of the absence of CEN. When rent depends on the location of residence (or, more realistically, depends on the company itself which has a fixed residence) inefficiencies are likely to occur because of the absence of CIN. Of course, these two possibilities are not mutually exclusive. As argued above, it seems likely that the absence of CEN may lead to a higher welfare loss than the absence of CIN. The absence of CIN generally corresponds to an absence of CEN at the individual portfolio level. This is the case if foreign shareholders are not discriminated against through withholding taxes or the unavailability of imputation tax credit. We therefore do not show the individual level separately.

The next three columns of Table 4.1 give some indication of the degree to which national governments need to give up sovereignty under potential reforms. 'Sovereignty' in Table 4.1 refers to the right of national governments to set their own tax regimes. All of the reforms considered allow for the possibility that both source and residence countries share the total tax revenue. Here we use a somewhat subjective grading system, giving a score of 10 to a system which allows the national government complete sovereignty and a score of zero to a system which leaves it with no sovereignty. 'Domestic' refers to operations which take place only in one country by a company resident in the same country. Table 4.2 addresses the issues under the other headings in the previous section: administrative costs for the countries concerned, and compliance costs for the companies, together with other factors.

The purpose of corporate tax harmonisation is to improve economic efficiency. Therefore the first reform considered is the one which most closely approaches the economic ideal. It is, however, very far from being politically acceptable, and the rest of the reforms progressively trade-off economic efficiency with political sovereignty and administrative simplicity.

(i) Single European Corporation Tax

This is clearly the most extreme form of harmonisation. Agreement would need to be reached on the tax base, the tax rate and whether to have an imputation, classical or split-rate system. Withholding taxes on payments of interest and dividends abroad would be abolished. Companies (or more precisely, groups) would simply be taxed on their total Europe-wide profits. Some allocation between member states of revenues generated would need to be introduced, possibly along the lines of unitary tax systems e.g. based on the size of the payroll, property and sales. Start-up losses could be offset against existing taxable profit as long as they were incurred somewhere in the European Community. (This could not easily be achieved with simply twelve identical tax systems.) If such a tax were introduced with an imputation system the tax credit would be available to any EC shareholder resident in a member state. Member states would, of course, be free to levy income tax on dividends at any rate in this as in all the reforms mentioned below.

Such a system clearly removes all intra-European economic inefficiencies due to differing corporate tax systems, which is its primary aim. In addition it reduces administrative and compliance costs since there is only one tax system, and transnational flows between parent and subsidiary can simply be netted out of the tax base. It also solves problems due to thin capitalisation and transfer pricing, for the same reason. Transnational mergers within Europe would not be discouraged. Even with all these advantages (which are gained whatever the regime is, so long as there is only one system), such a system must be considered unlikely simply because national governments would need to give up more sovereignty than they are probably prepared to (this may be one reason why the Commission's progress towards harmonisation has been so slow). Since as much sovereignty would need to be given up to have twelve identical tax systems, with a lesser gain in terms of economic and administrative efficiency, this option is not considered separately.

(ii) Corporate Tax in the Location of Shareholder Residence

This is the most complicated of the reforms considered in this chapter, but it provides one other way to achieve both CEN and CIN; it is a tax based on the regime operating in the country of residence of the shareholder. This would not involve the harmonisation of statutory tax rates or tax bases. However, it would imply that *full* credit must always be given for foreign taxes paid. The following example explains how this could work. Suppose a British resident owned shares in a French company which operated via a partly-owned subsidiary in Spain. First, the Spanish government would tax the subsidiary according to the Spanish tax system. The French government would then tax that part of the subsidiary's profits attributable to the French company according to the French system, giving full credit for Spanish tax already paid on that part of the profit. Some or all of the credit given could be reclaimed from Spain; the amount reclaimed could be left for bilateral negotiation between the two countries. The allocation of revenue can be separated from the setting of the tax rate and the collection of revenue. Note that under this system the French government charges tax irrespective of whether the profits are repatriated or not. However, the aim of this system is that the ultimate shareholder should end up paying the same underlying rate of tax on his or her investment irrespective of the country in which he or she invests it. When the French company pays dividends (with or without a tax credit on the dividend), the British government must charge tax at the full British corporate tax rate on the profit on which dividends are paid (including corporation tax, ACT and income tax i.e. 35 per cent for a basic rate taxpayer) giving full credit for French tax paid (a proportion of which can again be reclaimed from the French government, depending on bilateral agreement). If the French tax rate were greater than the UK tax rate, the UK shareholder would be entitled to a refund of tax on receipt of dividend.

What this rather complicated arrangement achieves is that, *ceteris paribus*, the owners of companies, the shareholders, are indifferent to where they invest their money since the effective rate of tax payable is independent of the location of the company in which shares are bought.[4] If companies act in the interests of their shareholders (regarding the relevant tax as the shareholder's, not the company's) then decisions at a corporate level will also be independent of tax. However, even if they ignore shareholder's tax, tax at the parent company level is independent of the location of the company's activities and so CEN is achieved. Also, however, returning to the Renault and Fiat example, the two companies can now compete on an equal footing since individual shareholders can buy shares in either, and so CIN is also achieved.[5]

This system has an advantage over a single European corporation tax in terms of loss of sovereignty. Under this system, national governments would retain sovereignty as regards taxing resident individual shareholders. This may be unimportant with respect to individuals investing in foreign companies, but is more significant for the majority of cases in which domestic companies are owned by domestic residents. However, the country in which production takes place and the country in which the parent company resides both need to give up sovereignty although both could continue to claim some revenue (but only a proportion of the tax charged elsewhere). Some disadvantages of the scheme are in administration and compliance. The country in which the parent company resides would need to compute the tax due on profit arising throughout Europe. The country of shareholder residence would also need to do the same, calculating the full amount of tax that would have been paid on the profit underlying any dividend. Issues such as transfer pricing and thin capitalisation are avoided since it only needs to calculate one aggregate tax base, and as the tax base is European profits rather than national profits, there are no start-up or merger problems.

(iii) Corporation Tax in the Parent Company Residence Location

This option is a simpler version of the previous one. Essentially it stops at the parent company level. Thus, using the same example of a Spanish company operating in Spain and partly owned by a French holding company, the Spanish government would first tax the operations taking place in Spain according to the Spanish tax system. As before, the French government would then tax that part of the

Spanish company's profits attributable to the French company according to the French tax system, giving full credit for Spanish tax already paid on that part of the profit.[6] Once again, there may be bilateral agreement between governments to allocate total revenues collected. Since the parent company faces the same tax rate on all its Europe-wide operations CEN is achieved. However, CIN is not achieved — Renault may face a higher tax rate than Fiat.

As discussed in Chapter 1, this absence of CIN may be viewed in some sense as a CEN problem at the portfolio investment level, since individuals may invest in Fiat rather than Renault if the overall tax rate faced on their returns will be lower. Hence the country in which individuals invest is affected by tax. This system could be operated with or without a European-wide imputation system such as that advocated by the Commission (1975). To the extent to which tax credits can be claimed by shareholders resident in a country other than that in which the productive activity takes place, then the shareholder CEN problem at the portfolio investment level is reduced. It should be noted that such CIN problems would be exacerbated if withholding taxes were payable by foreign portfolio shareholders on dividends paid to them, or if such shareholders were unable to claim the benefit of any imputation tax credits which they could claim elsewhere. These issues are unimportant at the holding company level under this reform where the residence country would in any case give full credit for all foreign taxes paid.

This system requires national governments to yield less sovereignty since they can set whatever tax system they like to apply to resident companies (including those which operate only domestically). National governments can also charge domestic shareholders of foreign companies any rate of income tax on their dividends (although by differing across countries this might exacerbate CIN problems depending on the extent to which companies take into account the taxes paid by individual shareholders). There is also one administrative advantage over the previous option in that the computation required by the country or residence of the shareholder is more straightforward. As the tax base continues to be European profits in total, with full credit for foreign tax, there are no merger, start-up, transfer pricing or thin capitalisation problems. In sum, charging corporation tax essentially on a residence basis of the parent company rather than of the shareholder gives up some economic efficiency in return for more sovereignty and fewer administrative problems.

(iv) Corporation Tax Mainly in the Parent Company Residence Location

The main political drawback of the previous option is probably that the government of the country in which production takes place (the source country) yields sovereignty. It may still claim a share of the tax revenue collected on profits made in its country but it will be a share of an amount determined under the tax system of the parent's residence country. If this were an insuperable drawback, a partial rather than full credit system could be used.[7] To some extent, this would work in the same way as the system currently in use in the UK, in that credit would be given in the residence country for the source country's tax only to the extent that it is no greater than the residence country's tax. However, it would differ from the current UK system insofar as the resident country would charge tax on Europe-wide profit, rather than just on repatriated dividends (and branch profit). As in the previous cases, the allocation of total revenue between the relevant countries could be a matter for negotiation. Note that this would complicate administration in the country of parent residence, because whereas under the previous option it simply calculates tax on European profits and gives credit for all tax paid, now it must compare the tax paid on the profits made in each member state with the domestic rate. An alternative would be for the residence country to pool all foreign tax paid and treat it as having borne an *average* rate of tax. This would probably involve lower administrative costs. However, overall this reform probably increases administration costs over the previous option, and it returns us to a situation in which transfer pricing and thin capitalisation potentially become tools for reducing the aggregate tax burden for a company.

An index of sovereignty is a very subjective exercise, but a figure of four out of ten would seem appropriate for the source country which can set a high tax rate, but not receive revenue except for what it gets from the excess of its tax rate over the residence country, plus what is agreed in any bilateral negotiations. The sovereignty of the resident country also is limited — it cannot set a low tax rate for the European-wide operations of its resident companies. Presumably this is not a great loss; a figure of seven reflects this.

This proposal therefore gives sovereignty back to the source country to the extent that it wishes to charge a high rate of tax (a low tax bill will be added to by the residence country). However, it does so at a cost of losing CEN. Companies will no longer be indifferent to the country in which they set up production plants, since in some countries they will face a higher charge than in others. Note, though, that a credit system with averaging would provide a system that was closer to CEN, since the disadvantage of investing in a high tax country would be reduced.

(v) Corporation Tax in the Parent Company Residence Location for Repatriations

So far only options in which Europe-wide profits are taxed as one entity have been considered. One drawback with such an approach (except under the single European tax) is that taxable profit must be computed for the same operation under two different tax codes (those of the source and residence country). The administrative and compliance costs involved in such computations must be one important reason why such schemes have not been introduced in Europe (although such schemes exist under the unitary tax systems of the US and Canada). The obvious way of reducing these costs would be for the residence country to tax only the repatriated dividends of resident-owned foreign subsidiaries, as is currently the case under most credit systems. There would then be the option of offering full credit or partial credit.

Under either a full credit or partial credit administration and compliance costs would be lower although, as under current systems, there would be problems of transfer pricing and thin capitalisation. Under a full credit system, the extent to which either the source or the residence country could determine the tax bill would depend on the proportion of profits repatriated. If all profits are repatriated, then we are essentially in case (iii) above, and the residence country chooses the tax system. If no profits are repatriated, then we have a source-based tax, with the source country choosing the tax system. Since this system can be similar to either a residence- or source-based tax, it does not have either of the economic efficiency qualities, CEN or CIN. Furthermore, an additional inefficiency is introduced via this system. That is that the decision whether or not to repatriate profits will depend on the tax system. As noted above, this is likely to have important effects. Looking at the sovereignty implications, it would seem that compared to the previous option, the source country has slightly more because it can tax retained earnings, and the residence country correspondingly less.

However, the results of Chapter 2 (Tables 2.7 and 2.8) showed that the simple reform of abolishing withholding taxes on dividends and interest paid abroad and the introduction of partial credit systems in each country constituted a significant improvement on the current situation in terms of *both* CEN and CIN.

(vi) Unitary Tax

Unitary tax is prevalent within the US and Canada. It was discussed in detail in Chapter 1 and only a brief summary will be given here. Translating a system common in US states to Europe would lead to a system in which each country taxed every company either operating, residing or selling in that country on a proportion of its Europe-wide taxable profits, as determined by that country's tax code. Clearly, if all countries had the same tax code and used the same apportionment formula, then this system is essentially that discussed above as a single European tax. By taxing Europe-wide profits, the problems of transfer pricing and thin capitalisation are avoided, as are the problems of start-up costs and mergers.

However, if countries maintain different tax codes, the benefits of a unitary tax system are much reduced. First, CEN is not achieved, since the country of production affects the total tax burden. CIN will, however, broadly be present. If Fiat just happens to be more efficient than Renault, but Italy has a higher effective unitary tax rate, this would only result in Fiat paying higher taxes than Renault insofar as it keeps buildings, work force and sales in Italy. All of these could be moved to France. Second, the administrative and compliance problems of a unitary tax system without harmonised tax bases are huge. Each company must calculate its Europe-wide taxable profits several times, the actual number depending on the number of countries in which it operates in some way. Each country's tax administration must check the Europe-wide profits of every company operating in some way within that country. It should be noted that the systems operating in North America have very similar tax bases in the different jurisdictions.

The sovereignty issue is more complex. Assuming the formula apportioning profits is based on work force and buildings, the source country will have jurisdiction over a large proportion of profits. The residence country would be worse-off, perhaps just having the group's head office and staff.

(vii) Corporation Tax in Location of Production

The options so far discussed began by examining tax systems based principally on a residence base (the tax system used was that of the country of residence of the holding company or shareholder). By relaxing various aspects of those systems we introduced elements of source country taxation (the tax system was that according to the country in which the activity takes place). Moving completely to source country taxation would generate CIN; *ceteris paribus*, Renault and Fiat would both operate in the lowest taxed country on an equal footing. However, it is clear that CEN would be lost. Clearly also, the residence country must yield sovereignty, although, again, it may claim a share of the tax collected by the source country, depending on bilateral negotiation.

A source based tax system has the advantage of being administratively simple, and easy to move to from the current system since all that is needed is the abolition of withholding taxes on the payment of dividends and interest abroad and the introduction of exemption from tax of foreign source income. The latter would be relatively costless as credit systems tend to yield little revenue. The former is a requirement of all the options discussed here. The abolition of withholding taxes is the reason why the source country would not have as much sovereignty as currently. Countries would lose the right to tax foreign owned companies more heavily than domestically owned companies. It should be noted, moreover, that the results in Tables 2.7 and 2.8 indicated that such a simple change from current regimes would yield large reductions in tax induced distortions in Europe.

4.4 Abolition of Withholding Taxes

The strategy followed in the previous section was to start from the European corporate tax system which was most efficient, and then to gradually trade off efficiency in favour of political sovereignty. However, there is another reform strategy, which is to examine the current situation and to see if any minimal reforms might improve European efficiency. The simplest way of improving economic efficiency within Europe is simply to abolish withholding taxes on the payment of dividends and interest abroad. At a company level, the existence of a withholding tax payable (or at least not rebateable) by foreigners eliminates the possibility of source based taxation, which requires that all companies investing in a particular country must face the same effective tax rate. A withholding tax clearly discriminates on the basis of the residence of the company. In cases in which there is a residence based location specific rent, then the existence of a withholding tax means that CIN cannot be achieved. In addition, to the extent that withholding taxes introduce discrimination between the effective tax rates faced by a company considering an investment in more than one country, it also means that CEN is not achieved. For these reasons withholding taxes are likely to introduce inefficiencies and hence a welfare loss. It might be noted that these consideration were clearly borne out by the results shown in Chapter 2, which indicated that a significant degree of distortion could be avoided by the abolition of such withholding taxes. This improvement in efficiency would be gained by a small reduction in the sovereignty of the source country (and probably also a small drop in its revenue). However, abolishing withholding taxes would not solve other problems which exist under the current system. It does not provide a blueprint of some ideal tax system, simply a better version of the current one.

It should also be noted that a closely related issue is the availability to foreign shareholders of a tax credit arising from an imputation system. If the foreign shareholder is in fact a parent company the same considerations apply as for the withholding tax. Extending the benefits of receiving such a credit may also help relieve another problem. In some countries, notably the UK, there is a constraint on companies in that ACT can only be set against corporation tax paid in that country. This imposes a degree of capital export non-neutrality if the company has unrelieved ACT as a result, since there would be a tax advantage to investing at home. An additional element of a minimal reform would therefore be to allow an imputation tax credit to be claimed in the residence country. (The government of the residence country would in turn claim the tax credit from the source country via a clearing system.) In this case, it could therefore be used under the UK system in the same way as dividends and the ACT tax credit received from subsidiaries within the UK.

Both withholding taxes and the non-availability of imputation tax credit may also apply to portfolio shareholders. As noted in Chapter 1, their existence implies an additional reason why CEN may not be achieved at the portfolio investment level, in addition to other distortions causing CIN. In principle then the abolition of withholding taxes and the availability of imputation tax credits should be extended to foreign portfolio investors.

4.5 The Role of Competitive Pressures

Whenever there is an element of taxation in the country of production against which full credit is *not* given, there may be competition between countries to attract foreign investment. For instance, if corporation tax were source based as in reform (vii), then where production location specific rents are low (in other words, the cost of production varies little according to the country of production) companies will locate in the lowest tax country. It is possible that the combination of the extra jobs, exports and corporate tax revenues that such inward investment brings may encourage countries to reduce the effective rate of corporation tax on inward investment (relative to outward investment).

Where tax is based on the country of company residence (reforms (iii), (iv) and (v) above, for instance) there may be pressure of a different sort. A foreign owned company, operating in the same market as a domestically owned company, may face a lower tax rate. There is some incentive for the domestic government to lower tax rates on domestic companies (and hence on their operations in other European countries) to eliminate this tax induced advantage.

It is possible to interpret some recent national reforms of corporate taxes as being responses to such pressures. It appears that the UK authorities think that formal harmonisation of corporation tax in the EC might not be necessary, because '... it remains to be demonstrated why market forces within the freer liberalised single market after 1992 will not by themselves be sufficient to bring about any necessary degree of convergence'. (J. Isaac, Deputy Chairman of the Board of Inland Revenue, 1989).

Several important points should be noted. Given these two possible aims of governments — to encourage net inward investment and to benefit domestically-owned companies relative to foreign ones — and given the structure of European taxes, it is not clear what the incentives for governments are. Even if the incentive were clear, governments would have to weigh the benefits of changing tax rates against the fact that they presumably wish to raise some revenue from corporate income. In fact, the incentives depend to a large degree on how other countries tax foreign source income. We consider three different cases — a source-based tax, a mainly residence-based tax, and a structure largely as at present.

If withholding taxes are abolished and all countries have exemption systems, each country would have an incentive to increase (or maintain) net inward investment by cutting effective tax rates in its country. The danger with this is that the equilibrium point reached in this 'competitive market' may be with zero or even negative tax revenue. It is possible that countries would need to offer higher and higher incentives to maintain their existing net inward investment.

To some extent there is evidence of countries adopting this competitive undercutting approach even now — Luxembourg, by reducing its indirect taxes, has become a sort of duty free shop for the inhabitants of neighbouring states. Some countries have given substantial discretionary grants in order to encourage particular investments to depressed regions of their own countries. It would be very difficult to legislate against this; in the case of indirect taxes it has been argued (Lee, Pearson and Smith, 1988) that a minimum tax rate should be set for those countries and goods where there might be a problem. In the case of corporation taxes, a minimum tax rate would be useless without specification of a minimum base, and so even in this setting a minimum it would be necessary to limit member states' sovereignty. However, it is possible that legislation may not be necessary simply because each country will need to trade-off additional inward investment against lower revenue, both from the inward investment and from the remaining domestic investment.

Incentives for the source country would be somewhat different if partial credit systems were adopted in all member states. In the absence of withholding taxes, there would be no gain from having the lowest effective tax rate and only minimal gain from having the next lowest rate. This is because the residence country would simply add to the tax liability. The incentive for source countries is therefore more to avoid having a high tax rate;[8] this suggests a movement towards harmonisation rather than undercutting. For residence countries, however, there may still be some incentive to set a low effective tax rate on domestically-operating companies in order to give them a competitive advantage over foreign companies. To the extent that this is important, there will again be a potential undercutting. Given that all countries are, in fact, both source and residence countries, the structure of incentives for governments is unclear.

If withholding taxes continue to exist, the pressure to change tax rates is still more confused. If partial credit systems are generally in place, for example, then there is an incentive for countries to set low general corporate tax rates but large withholding taxes. The withholding tax would capture for the source country the main share of the tax revenue on operations by foreign companies in that country (which would otherwise be taxed by the residence country), while the low general tax rate would benefit domestically-operating companies. It is clear that, in this case (which is very close to the current system[9]) countries have incentives to act in such a way that CIN, at least, becomes less likely.

In general, although corporate tax systems in Europe have apparently been moving closer together, the evidence from Chapter 2 suggests that they remain a long way apart. It seems that so far competitive pressures have *not* resulted in harmonisation. It might, perhaps, be argued that further movement is likely in the single European market post-1992 when there should be fewer other distortions to competition. However, it is not the case that the belief in the power of market forces to induce some degree of harmonisation should imply that the Commission and national governments should do nothing. This is both because the evidence to date suggests that distortions are still present, and because considerable reductions in those distortions could be achieved with relatively small changes to European corporate tax regimes. These changes, moreover, would maintain most of the sovereignty of national governments to design their own regimes.

Hence 'market-led' movement towards harmonisation might be a blessing, bringing CEN closer where institutional arrangements ensure CIN, or vice versa, but it is possible that it may be double-edged, resulting in the general tax rate being lower than that which many and possibly all member states would prefer.

4.6 Conclusions

Two strong conclusions emerge from this discussion. The first is that proposals for harmonisation are more likely to be acceptable, and more likely to achieve the goal of economic efficiency, if they are directed towards the taxation of transnational flows rather than domestic tax rates and bases. This suggests that the direction in which the Commission appears to be moving — proposing a harmonised tax base, rates and imputation system — is both largely unnecessary and likely to remain on the table for some considerable time without being accepted by member states.

The second strong conclusion is that withholding taxes on the payment of dividends and interest abroad should be abolished since they are detrimental to the efficiency of the European economy to an extent disproportionate to the revenue they raise. The same applies to tax credits available under imputation systems. As proposed by the Commmission in 1975, tax credits should be available to foreign shareholders.

Beyond these conclusions there is more scope for disagreement, depending on the importance attached to the various criteria outlined above. However, of the options discussed above, three seem to us to stand out as being reasonable compromises between the various criteria. The first, which is our preferred reform, would be option (iii), with corporation tax essentially being levied under the tax system of the country of residence of the parent company. This achieves one of our main economic objectives, CEN, while maintaining full sovereignty for the residence country, principally at the cost of a loss of sovereignty for the government of the source country (although this does *not* mean that the source country cannot share in the revenue collected, nor that the source country cannot maintain its own tax system for its domestic activities). This option also requires some change from the existing methods of taxing transnational flows and implies some increase in administrative and compliance costs. A weaker version of this reform is option (iv) which returns some sovereignty to the same country at the loss of some CEN.

Two methods of improving matters while implementing only limited change would be options (v) and (vii). Option (v) is very similar to the UK system in that withholding taxes on the payment of dividends and interest abroad are abolished, and the residence country taxes repatriations of profit under a partial credit system. This option does not strictly achieve CEN or CIN. However, the results in Chapter 2 indicate that economic distortions would be considerably reduced. In addition administrative and compliance costs remain low.

Option (vii) essentially introduces source country taxation, by abolishing witholding taxes and introducing exemption systems for the taxation of foreign source income. While largely maintaining sovereignty for the source country, this reduces the right of residence countries to tax foreign source income (although very little revenue is raised in this manner under current systems). This option also maintains low administrative and compliance costs. Concerning economic objectives, it achieves CIN since companies resident in all countries can move their activities to the same low-taxed country. The results of Chapter 2 indicate also that CEN would be brought closer.

To the extent that either of these options is adopted there may be competitive pressure on national governments to harmonise their corporate tax systems still further, which would, in either case, lead to CEN being more nearly achieved.

NOTES

1. As noted in Chapter 1, CIN is sometimes used to refer to the case where different companies *investing* in a particular country, rather than selling in a particular country, face the same effective marginal tax rate (see Musgrave, 1987). This seems a less interesting case, except for those goods which cannot be exported.
2. The welfare loss would also be avoided if Renault could change its residence to Italy. Generally, changing residence is very difficult, as described in Chapter 1. A rather novel

way of ensuring a significant increase in capital import neutrality would be to permit companies to change their residence. However, this is probably politically impossible, and may in any case lead to a wasteful tax-cutting competition.

3. These issues are discussed in more detail in Chapter 1.

4. Note that this would not be achieved simply by allowing imputation tax credits to be claimed by foreign shareholders.

5. At least to the extent that companies aim to maximise the wealth of their shareholders.

6. There would probably need to be a *de minimis* rule, so that very small holdings in foreign companies were not taxed by the residence country of the holding company.

7. A full credit system involves refunding tax if the company has already paid in excess of that which it would have paid had the profits been generated domestically, as well as imposing an additional tax had the company paid too little. A partial credit only ever adds to a company's tax bill; it does not refund extra tax.

8. Note that Ireland is currently an exception to this rule. It has very low tax rates and very generous depreciation allowances; the result is that many investments in Ireland are subsidised — the effective marginal tax rate is negative. However, under bilateral agreements other countries treat the tax as being higher than it actually is. Ireland is, of course, on the Atlantic periphery of Europe, and so the impact of the low tax rates may always be limited.

9. The current system is complicated still further by the existence of exemption systems in some countries.

REFERENCES

Alworth, J.S. (1988), *The Financial, Investment and Taxation Decisions of Multinationals.* Oxford: Blackwell's.

Cecchini, P. (1988), *The European Challenge: 1992, the Benefits of a Single Market.* Aldershot: Wildwood House.

Chown, J. (1989), *Tax Harmonisation in Europe.* London: Institute of Directors.

Cnossen, S. (1989), 'How much tax harmonisation in the European Community?' in M. Gammie and B. Robinson (eds.) *Beyond 1992: A European Tax System.* Institute for Fiscal Studies Commentary no. 13.

Commission of the European Community (1967), *Programme for the Harmonisation of Direct Taxes.* Brussels: EC.

— (1969a), 'Draft Directive concerning the Common System of Taxation applicable in the case of mergers, divisions and contributions of assets taking place between corporations of different member states'. COM(69) 5 final.

— (1969b), 'Draft Directive concerning the Common System of Taxation applicable in the case of parent corporations and subsidiaries of different member states'. COM(69) 6 final.

— (1975), 'Draft Directive concerning the harmonisation of systems of company taxation and of withholding tax on dividends'. *Official Journal of the European Communities* no. C253. COM(75) 392 final.

— (1976), 'Draft Directive on the elimination of double taxation in connection with the adjustment of transfers of profits between associated enterprises (arbitration procedure)'. *Official Journal of the European Communities* C301.

— 1980, 'Report on the scope for convergence of tax systems in the Community', *Bulletin of the European Communities* Supplement 1/80.

— (1984), 'Draft Directive on the tax arrangements for the carry-over of losses of undertakings'. *Official Journal of the European Communities* numbers C253 1984 and C170 1985. COM(84) 404 final.

— (1988a), 'Preliminary Draft proposal for a directive on the harmonisation of rules concerning the taxable profits of undertakings'. XV/27/88.

— (1988b), 'Commission communication on the method for the application of Article 92 (3) (a) and (c) to regional aid'. *Official Journal of the European Communities,* C212, volume 31.

— (1989),'Un Statut pour des Enterprises a la Dimension de 1992'. COM(89) 268.

Coopers and Lybrand (1988), *International Tax Summaries — A Guide for Planning and Decisions.* London: Coopers and Lybrand.

Crooks, E., Devereux, M., Pearson, M. and Wookey, C. (1989),'Transnational tax rates and incentives to invest'. IFS Working Paper no. 89/8.

European Regional Incentives (1988), *Review and Directory of Regional Incentives in the Member States of the European Community and Sweden.* Glasgow: European Policies Research Centre, University of Strathclyde.

Hines, J. R. and Hubbard, R. G. (1989), 'Coming home to America: dividend repatriations by US multinationals'. National Bureau of Economic Research, Inc. Working Paper No. 2931.

International Bureau of Fiscal Documentation (1988), *The Taxation of Companies in Europe. Guides to European Taxation: volume II.* Amsterdam: IBFD.

Isaac, J. (1989), 'Corporate tax harmonisation', in M. Gammie and B. Robinson (eds.) *Beyond 1992: A European Tax System.* Institute for Fiscal Studies Commentary no. 13.

King, M.A., and Fullerton, D. (eds.) (1984), *The Taxation of Income from Capital; A Comparative Study of the United States, the United Kingdom, Sweden, and West Germany.* Chicago: University of Chicago Press.

Lee, C., Pearson, M. and Smith, S. (1988), *Fiscal Harmonisation: an Analysis of the European Commission's Proposals.* IFS Report Series no. 28.

McClure Jr., C.E. (1989), 'European integration and taxation of corporate income at source: lessons from the US' in M. Gammie and B. Robinson (eds.) *Beyond 1992: A European Tax System.* Institute for Fiscal Studies Commentary no. 13.

Musgrave, P.B. (1987) 'Interjurisdictional coordination of taxes on capital income', in Cnossen, S. (ed.), *Tax Coordination in the European Community.* London: Kluwer Law and Taxation Publishers.

Neumark Committee (1963), 'Report of the Fiscal and Financial Committee' in *Tax Harmonisation in the Common Market*. Chicago: Commerce Clearing House.

Organisation for Economic Co-operation and Development (1988a), *Revenue Statistics of OECD Member Countries 1966-1985*. Paris: OECD.

— (1988b), *Thin Capitalisation*. Paris.

— (1989), *Tax Obstacles: Quantification of Corporate Tax Rates (Note by the Secretariat)*. Restricted circulation. Paris.

Pearson, M. and Smith, S. (1988), *Opening up the Tax Frontiers, a report prepared for the European Roundtable of Industrialists*. Brussels: European Roundtable of Industrialists.

Price Waterhouse (1988), *Corporate Taxes: A Worldwide Summary*. London: Price Waterhouse.

Times (1989), *The Times 1000 1988-1989: The World's Top Companies*. London: Times Books.

Touche Ross International (1989), *Tax and Investment Profile*. (various countries).

Van den Tempel, A.J. (1971), *Corporation Tax and Individual Income Tax in the European Communities*. Brussels: Commission of the European Community.

THE INSTITUTE FOR FISCAL STUDIES

REPORT SERIES

Recent titles include:

Alcohol Consumption and Taxation
Edmund Crooks (1989)

The Monopolies Commission and the Market Process
Richard Shaw and Paul Simpson

Who Pays Indirect Taxes?
Catherine Lee and Panos Pashardes (1988)

Local Income Tax: Options for the Introduction of a Local Income Tax in
the United Kingdom
John Kay and Stephen Smith (1988)

Fiscal Harmonisation: An Analysis of the European Commission's
Proposals
Catherine Lee, Mark Pearson and Stephen Smith (1988)

Reports are available to non-members at £10 each

COMMENTARIES

Recent titles include:

Beyond 1992: a European Tax System
Malcolm Gammie and Bill Robinson (eds.) (1989)   £7.50

Taxation and Social Security 1979-1989: The Impact on Household Incomes
Paul Johnson and Graham Stark (1989)   £6

Death: the Unfinished Business
Second Report of the Capital Taxes Group (1988)   £6

Privatising Electricity: Impact on the UK Energy Market
Bill Robinson (ed.) (1988)   £6

Reforming Capital Gains Tax
Interim Report of the Capital Taxes Group (1988)   £6

*If you would like a list of earlier Commentaries and Reports or details of our Working
Papers please write to the IFS at 180 Tottenham Court Road, London W1P 9LE*